Books, Bandits and Guns

ONE MAN'S WAR IN SOMALIA

by

TIM MOORE

and

DAVID MOORE

THE CHOIR PRESS

First published in the United Kingdom in 2017 by
The Choir Press

ISBN 978-1-911589-05-1

Books, Bandits
and Guns

❧⌣⌣☙

White Nile

Blue Nile

Adis Abba

**ABYSSINIA
(Ethiopia)**

SOMALILAND

Dagabur

OGADEN

Imi

Danan

SOMALIA

Uebi Scebeli

UGANDA

KENYA

Kampala

Nakuru

R. Tana

Garissa

R. Juba

Mogadishu

Lake
Victoria

Nairobi

Kismayu

Arusha

Present Day Border
1941-1944 Border

Mombasa

TANGANYIKA

Zanzibar

INDIAN

Dodoma

Dar es Salaam

Iringa

Mbeya

**Northern
Rhodesia
(Zambia)**

N
Y
A
S
A
L
A
N
D

OCEAN

MOZAMBIQUE

Zomba

R. Zambesi

**Southern
Rhodesia
(Zimbabwe)**

Beira

MADAGASCAR

Eastern Africa & Madagascar

Contents

ം∽∿∽ം

Tim Moore

To the sweetest girl of all (Freda), from Tim

Part 1

PREFACE TO PART 1

∽✿∽

I must apologise for any inconsistencies in this story. Should any emergency similar to it occur again, I would advise any young soldier never heedlessly to respond without due thought to any call for volunteers. They should not fight in any army splinter groups such as the Eritrean Volunteers, the British Military Mission to Ethiopia or the Somalia Gendarmerie. Having done so, it is difficult to withdraw without loss of face – and applications for transfers always seem to get lost, ignored or rejected.

The struggle to find peace amongst the Somalis continued after our involvement and it was not until the deplorable misery of the starving people in the drought and famine that it came to Western notice. The American Army force attempted to help and bring aid. The US Army tried to make a landing which was repelled in 1993, since when Somalia ceased to make the headlines. This was when I was inspired to collect together my scraps of torn and faded papers to see if a coherent narrative of my experiences in Somalia could be formed. The tattered sheets and a school exercise book some fifty years old have been collected together from memorabilia.

My memories of the Somalis and Arabs of the Ogaden are of a charming, fine, handsome, brave and religious people.

In regard to the narrative, apologies are tendered for what might seem to be minor errors of time and place due to age, defective sight and wear and tear of tattered old papers.

Finally, I am often asked why, if my first name is Simeon, I am called 'Tim'. When I was born on 25th May 1911, it was suggested it would differentiate me from my father of the same name.

S J Moore
Ringwood, Hampshire

1

Recollections of Nairobi Life

❦

I think the best place for me to start is when I was lying on my bunk in His Highness the Sultan of Zanzibar's good ship, the *Al Said*. The steel deck was about a foot above my head. It was intolerably hot as the little ship pitched and tossed in the Indian Ocean, on our voyage from Mombasa to Mogadishu, while the sickly smell of the retching of the sea sick askari came up from the lower deck.

It was a tiny steam ship which in the good old days used to carry produce and a few carpets and passengers between the Persian Gulf, Mombasa and Zanzibar. Strange that it should now be used against the might of Hitler and Mussolini. Griffiths Stevenson was on the lower bunk and Michael Finnegan, a superintendent from the Tanganyika Police Force, lay on the deck below as it was only a two-berth cabin.

Between dozing and waking, I wondered what was going to happen to us and contemplated the events which had led up to our pitching and tossing in that little grey and white cockle shell – my childhood in Nairobi; how I used to play barefoot with the little Kikuyus; how when I was about seven years old (about 1918), I was taken to the big school where lots of boys, both big and little, were all mixed up. They arrived at school, some driven in their parents' rickety Tin Lizzies (Model T Fords), others pulled in rickshaws, yet others on horseback and some merely walking there as I did. The school consisted of a number of flimsy corrugated iron buildings outside which the boys all congregated, until the clanking of the bell called them into the largest cedar-lined corrugated iron shed, which served as a hall for morning assembly and prayers.

'Nyrobi', as the railway men first spelled it, came into existence on 30th May 1899 when the rails of the Uganda Railway reached a piece of swampy ground, called by the Masai 'Uase en-airobe' ('the place of cold water'), on the edge of the Kikuyu Forest. A railhead was established, on the last bit of flat ground, to gather men and materials for the assault on the highlands and the formidable obstacle of the Great Rift Valley. Here the railway workshops, sheds, marshalling yards, headquarters and staff housing were established, and very soon other buildings were built round the railway station to become the embryo Nairobi.

My father, also Simeon James Moore, did not like the atmosphere in South Africa after the Boer War, so he came to Kenya in 1914 with a wife (Mercy) and two children (myself and Phoebe) and about £50 in his pocket. The East African Standard Bookshop was already established in Nairobi, but they had had a rather unfortunate fire and my father went in temporarily to help them with their troubles.

He established his own bookselling business in 1915 – 'S J Moore' – but the war had broken out and he was conscripted into the army, leaving his wife to run the business. During his intermittent returns to Nairobi from German East Africa on leave, he worked in the bookshop and did what organisation he could until the time that he was demobbed.

The business suffered many vicissitudes during the post-war depression. Nairobi was mainly a shanty town and the only stone building in Government Road was Nairobi House. The rest were, for the most part, wood and iron. In two very large fires most of Government Road and some of Harding Street was completely razed to the ground. S J Moore Ltd was completely burnt out during the first fire and, having moved its premises, was then burnt out again during the second fire. Due to unforeseen insurance technicalities, my father lost a considerable amount of money after the first fire. After the second fire, he was rather more sophisticated and did not lose any insurance payments through technicalities, although he did not recover from the shock of the first fire.

We lived in a wooden and iron house in Bishops Road and over the years three more children were born – Margie, Harry and Ruth. Most of the houses in those early days were built on wooden frames, outwardly protected by corrugated iron and inside tastefully panelled with local cedar and other timbers. The whole was supported on stone pillars, cupped on top with zinc iron sheeting which gave protection against being eaten by white ants. We called them termites and they would devour any timbers except the aromatic red cedar woods.

4

Government Road, Nairobi, circa 1915. The large building on the right, Cearns Nairobi House, was remarkable in that it had that wonder – a lift. In the foreground is a 'hamil' cart, quite a profitable local transporter. The dark building in the middle was later demolished, replaced by Barclays Bank. The askari (native policeman) standing in the road under the shop signboard wore khaki shorts, red cummerbund and tall red fez. The signboard read 'Moolchands' (Indian jeweller's). The signboard on the white roof, just above the little girl, proudly reads 'S J Moore, Bookseller'.

Later, after a disastrous fire, most of the crude wooden and corrugated iron shops were gutted. Some stocks, including salvaged books, were thrown onto the pavement. During the conflagration, it was said that bullets were exploding out of the two gun shops, H May and Chas Heyer. On the left, the lady wearing a topee could have been my mother, while the gentleman on the right in a suit and white helmet was no doubt my father.

Early Government Road. The shop is now built in stone and motor cars have arrived.

Outside the bathroom was a galvanised iron water tank which piped hot water, heated by a roaring fire of eucalyptus logs, into the bathroom.

Here Nairobi grew up on the edge of the uplands where the Athi Plains met the more luscious highlands. Almost anything could be grown here, and the place was a teeming land of natural flora together with large and small animals. During periods of drought, lions used to come into the town at night looking for water dribbling from outside taps, and many a housewife looking through her window in the early dawn was startled to see a huge lion or lioness on her garden lawn. Dogs could not be let out at night for fear of being taken by leopards, but our domestic cat seemed well able to look after herself.

When I was a small boy and sent to bed early I often did not go to sleep immediately. I was able to hear some of the gossip of the small town in which very few ramshackle motor cars drove along the main road, blowing up clouds of red dust. A friendly neighbour would jovially remark about the diminutive little men who ran a transport business in competition with the well-established Ali Khan, who used mule carts and took orders in an open space almost opposite the Norfolk Hotel: what an enterprise! They called themselves the ODTAA (One Damned Thing After Another) Transport. It made

The family. Left to right: *Margie, mother Mercy, Tim, Ruth, Harry, father Sim and Phoebe.*

everyone laugh. The Blaydon Taylors were so diminutive that they became known as the 'mighty atoms'!

The chatterers continued, unaware that a small boy was all ears. 'Didn't that fat old Mrs So-and-So look disgraceful in trousers this morning? Wish she could see herself. And flies! What on earth could she want flies for? Oh, and Hoppy Marshall, he went into a shop this morning and shouted, "Who the bloody hell left their car behind mine so that I can't get out?" A cultured voice answered, "That is my car. Don't you know me? I'm Lady Betty Walker of Tree Tops, Nyeri." Hoppy retorted, "And do you know who I am? I'm 'oppy Marshall, the public 'angman. Now go and move your car."'

Soon I would awake to the pleasant clinking of teacups as parents drank their 'cuppas' dosed with pinches of Epsom salts, or later Kruschen salts. 'One cannot be too careful in the tropics.' Meanwhile, the 'boy', as African domestic servants were called, was preparing the breakfast of lamb chops, bacon and eggs.

In the early days Nairobi was a shanty, Wild West kind of town. The Cecil Davis and Medicks families ran the only cinema, the Theatre

Royal. New films from England arrived at irregular intervals of weeks or months and often something went wrong with the projector, or there were power cuts, and we demanded our money back. There was not much entertainment, but there was fun. Between evening sundowners (there is a little twilight on the Equator), beery sunburned farmers in town for the evening, or night, arranged rickshaw races in the late evening or early dawn, urging their black pullers to their utmost.

There was a quaint wooden and iron hotel called the Stanley Hotel. One evening somebody put a bomb in it and blew it across the road. The nice New Stanley Hotel was established from modest beginnings some time after that and lives on with its Thorntree Lounge. There were few pavements or kerbs and the open drains were a danger to temperate people, let alone to the many drunken revellers.

Initially, as there was no water-borne sewerage system, buckets were used as toilets. At night gangs of municipal African employees emptied the lavatory buckets from trap doors in the back walls of houses all along the streets. On one occasion, when a neighbour wanted to pay a call in the night, a burly black arm entered the trap door and, in a flash, pulled the bucket out, emptied and returned it – just in time! A joke was enjoyed by a young Mr Oxford who removed the pin from the axle on the wheel of an ox-drawn sanitary cart. As the vehicle ran down the hill the wheel came off, turning the cart over and spilling the contents into an important person's garden.

Indian traders, originally coolies brought over from India as labourers to build the Uganda Railway, sat cross-legged in their open-fronted shops in Bazaar Street surrounded by piles of rice and spices on trays on the cement floors. The aroma was strongly curried! Opposite, a wealthy Indian immigrant had secured a large open space where he cultivated the charming Jeevanjee Gardens in which he erected a statue of the Empress, Queen Victoria.

Meanwhile, the elderly letter writer sat with oriental patience under the pepper tree outside the post office with his little table, ink bottle and stationery, waiting for his next client. He would take dictation of family news from the client and scribe a letter, and possibly enclose money, to send to equally illiterate relatives in India.

There was pleasure and rejoicing when it was announced that Edward, the Prince of Wales, was about to visit the protectorate which was later to become Kenya Colony. Bunting, as much as was available, festooned the earthen dusty streets, which were regularly dampened by water carts drawn by old-fashioned steam engines, followed by steam rollers.

A flagstaff was erected in the town centre. Next morning a joker cheerfully cried, 'Look what some bloody fool has done.' There it was – a chamber pot, crowning the top! As no superstitious African or high-born Patel would touch such an item, an enterprising Jewish contractor came along and, summing up the situation, smilingly called for a ladder and uncrowned it, to many cheers from the onlookers.

In 'Wild West' Nairobi, hunters foregathered. Gunsmiths and taxidermists exhibited samples of their artistry in their shop windows, much to the wonder of the indigenous tribal residents. Beautiful hides of hyrax, leopards and other animals were freely on sale and years later, when restrictions were placed on the sale of skins, many an old resident bemoaned not having secured a hyrax rug or fine leopard skin coat.

Hunters, known locally as 'White Hunters', established businesses arranging hunting parties for wealthy Americans and other overseas tourists. Some became colourful, almost legendary figures of whom many stories were told. One, Alan Black, became very well known, as

Off to the zoo? Some animals, like this giraffe, were given new lives away from Africa.

9

did Bud Cottar, a jovial North American, who always supported his trousers with coloured braces. When his leg was being pulled, he joked that once when he was being charged by a wounded lioness, his gun got jammed, and at this crucial moment his braces gave way, his trousers fell down and the shocked lioness turned tail and scooted off into the bushes – possibly to lie in wait under cover, lest he try to follow and put an end to her wounds.

In an effort to get into conversation with Alan Black in the bar, a young tenderfoot said, 'Tell me about elephants. I have heard it said that there are elephant graveyards.'

'That's right,' replied the old bushwhacker. 'And do you know they are able to commit suicide? Well, they just put their trunks up their backsides and blow their brains out!'

Of course, there were the aristocratic lords and ladies in the town from the up-country areas of Nanyuki, Naivasha and Kinangop, known as the 'Happy Valley Set'. Among them were a sprinkling of 'remittance men', said to be paid allowances to stay away from home and not disgrace their family names in England. Graffiti on the walls in Nairobi exclaimed, 'Are you married, or do you live in Kenya?' and 'Born in the UK – strong in the head, weak in the arm. Born in Kenya – weak in the head, strong in the arm.'

When Captain B W L Nicholson, RN was appointed by the Colonial Office in England to take up the appointment of headmaster of the Nairobi Sixth Form School (later renamed the Prince of Wales School), a flagstaff was erected on the grassy quadrangle where, before assembly in the mornings, the Union flag was raised to a bugled reveille and lowered in the evenings to the retreat. The original shanty school grew and grew until magnificent new buildings were acquired a bit further out on the Lower Kabete hill. The boys were said to be turned out more English than the English. That being said, it was not until Jack Cohen had accidentally shot Willie Hall that the staff forbade students bringing their arms and ammunition to school.

They were self-reliant boys, many of whom had shot a Tommy (Thomson's gazelle), zebra, eland, or even a lion. In fact, when a patrol of selected boy scouts was sent to the International Jamboree at the Wembley Exhibition, Bill Ryan, whom the press had discovered had shot a number of lions by the time he was fifteen, became quite a celebrity and had his picture in the newspapers.

The great event of the term was when the boys and the 'heifers' from the girls' high school met on the train going home at the end of term. The only secondary schools for European children from Kenya, Uganda and Tanganyika were located in Nairobi. Those heading 'up-country' travelled on the 'School Special', which carried the pupils from Nairobi to the highlands, across the Great Rift Valley, up to Timboroa Summit at 9,136 feet (the highest railway in the British Empire), across the Equator and on to Uganda, terminating in Kampala, where it would arrive next day (on the same schedule as the mail train), depositing pupils at whatever station was nearest their home.

The authorities got to know about the hijinks which went on in that train and decided that the girls should go on a separate train. This caused despondency among the boys until they remembered that when there was an infestation of locust hoppers on the line, this caused the locomotive to slip and stall on the steep gradient on the line. Some tins of motor grease were obtained and applied to the rails in the path of the next girls' train, and so they were able to have some happy chats with their girl friends, before the track was cleaned and the locomotive managed to get the train on the move again. Sadly the boys were prevented from repeating the activity in the future!

Education standards became high, particularly when later 'Old Nick' was succeeded by a Mr 'Pink Percy' Fletcher, under whom the Prince of Wales School was claimed to be the only public school in the Empire outside England to receive a mention of excellence of education in *Whitaker's Almanack*.

Meanwhile, developments in the British East Africa Protectorate had progressed routinely, and in 1920, after the boundary with Uganda was redrawn, it became the Colony and Protectorate of Kenya. The protectorate was a strip of land ten miles inland from the coast and extending from the border of Tanganyika to Lamu, almost to the Somali border. The Sultan of Zanzibar had previously held all of what was British East Africa, and now it was reduced to this ten-mile strip. (Much later, in 1963, he even lost this, but that is another story altogether!)

The Uganda Railway, later renamed the Kenya Uganda Railway, was built from Mombasa on the coast to Kisumu on Lake Victoria, largely to open up the country and to abolish slave trade through Zanzibar to

Arabia. This opened up avenues of employment to suitably qualified school leavers.

A 'White Highlands' area was reserved specifically for white farmers, residents and business settlers of European origin, and it was the start of continuing complaints from the coolies who had helped build the railway. In the main shopping street in Nairobi, Government Road, there was a line of fine shops, mostly owned by Europeans. Gradually one by one they dropped out and were replaced by Indian traders until almost the whole street was taken over. My parents continued to struggle on in their shop with their loyal staff members. Their old wooden and galvanised corrugated iron bungalow was encased in beautiful blue quarried Kenya stone. It, together with other houses in the area, had a septic tank built in the garden and flush lavatories became commonplace, thus doing away with bucket collection by the night soil man!

Enterprising farmers introduced wheat, tea, coffee, sisal and later pyrethrum. Grahame Bell at Ruaraka, a place just outside Nairobi, imported many vegetables and fruit plants never before grown in Kenya's rich red soils. The Agricultural Department introduced other

Government Road later, showing increased traffic. The building with the clock tower is the mosque of the Ismaili community of which the Aga Khan is president.

The opposite side of Government Road. The bookshop was near the tall, dark building.

new plants and trees such as the eucalyptus, which in places quite changed the look of the landscape.

Following my school days I trained as a laboratory assistant at the veterinary laboratories which were established at Kabete near Nairobi, from 1st July 1928 to 30th April 1930, which I enjoyed immensely. However, my parents needed help, and I left to join the family bookshop.

To increase my knowledge in the trade I went to England and I gained some experience of bookselling by working in W H Smith & Son at Hambledon House, Portugal Street and various other branches. I got to love London with its dense fogs and hidden mysteries. There, I lodged with Mrs Russell, in Holland Park, West London, and met her daughter Freda, who was a scholarship pupil at the Godolphin and Latymer School. A few years later Freda was to come to Kenya and become my wife.

After this training I returned to work in my family bookshop, once a thriving business until Kenya was shattered by the pre-war world trade slump. Farmers were among their best customers but now could not pay their accounts. Everything, even newspapers, was always bought 'on tick'. They moaned, 'If only the price of coffee or sisal would go up a

The bookshop was later sold to E J Arnold, Educational Publishers, Leeds, but eventually came under the control of the Indian Text-Book Centre.

Interior of the shop. The date on the calendar is 1st January 1930.

The Jamia Mosque. Whilst it was being built a school friend and I used to climb the winding stairs to the tops of the minarets. The white building in the background is the Municipal Market.

Delamere Avenue leading to Valley Road in the distance, where the Nairobi Cathedral is under construction on the left.

few pounds!' Cattle and sheep could not be sold. It was reported in the newspapers that elsewhere in the world, such as Mexico, producers were using unsaleable products such as sisal and cotton to run their railway shunting engines. There were occasional suicides and the unemployed were shipped back to the UK as 'distressed British subjects', presumably to join the rest of the down-and-outs in England.

After waiting month after disappointing month for my salary and my father saying, 'Tim, we have to pay the staff's wages first,' I saw an advertisement in the *East African Standard* for a clerk at the headquarters of the King's African Rifles and Local Forces. I applied and, after a brief examination and production of acceptable references (I was at the time secretary of the All Saints Cathedral Committee), I was engaged on August 17th, 1937. My first task was to notify the other applicants that they were unsuccessful!

On the 12th November 1935 the newspaper seller is standing in front of the McMillan Memorial Library with, to the right, the Municipal Market and the Jamia Mosque. The Italians under Mussolini had invaded Abyssinia (Ethiopia) and, in order to put a stop to the invasion, the League of Nations proposed a ban on weapons sales and to put sanctions on rubber and metal, which took six weeks to organise. Three countries refused to apply them and oil was not included in these sanctions. Italy ignored the League and continued with the invasion of Abyssinia. This failure of the League of Nations led to its demise, and the Second World War was inevitable. The following chapters in this book describe some of the activities following these actions in Eastern Africa.

2

Army Service

⟨≈⌣⌣≈⟩

'So you want to be a soldier,' said the brigade major, Lieutenant Colonel P G Wodehouse, and he explained that the work entailed familiarisation with top-secret defence files: 'very much hard work.' I would be required, after having been vetted, to sign an undertaking in connection with the Official Secrets Act. All carbon papers and other drafts used during the day were to be burnt under strict supervision and absolutely nothing was to be discussed.

I became thoroughly acquainted with the files and the Kenya Defence Scheme, under a Lieutenant Kent. I walked or drove to work along the Gymkhana Road which ran between the Nairobi Club and the officers' messes and the KAR (King's African Rifles) lines.

Before the war there had been conscription of all able-bodied European settlers into the Kenya Defence Force with annual camps, obligatory weekly training and target shooting on the rifle ranges, initially presumably to deal with any internal unrest. Much later, in about 1937, the Kenya Regiment was formed from volunteers, largely under the enthusiasm of a Colonel Dunstan Adams, agreeing to undergo further strenuous training to become commissioned officers at the outbreak of hostilities. We were drilled by strict non-commissioned officers from well-known British regiments. Among the foremost of them was RSM Cummins, 'Big Jimmy', and later all came under the command of Lieutenant Colonel Lord Stratheden.

The Northern Brigade, the King's African Rifles and local forces were then under command of Brigadier Campbell, dubbed by his officers the 'Blood Orange' after his florid complexion. We were all a bit scared of him, and I more so when I went into his office first thing in the mornings to empty his out tray, only to find his dog lying in it. 'Go on,' WOI David Dewar, office superintendent, used to say. 'Give

On manoeuvres, Namanga, 1939.

Warrant Officer Class II Tim Moore, 1939.

18

the bloody thing a kick in the ribs.' Of all things – the Brigadier's dog? Anyway, as other officers gradually turned up to work, some with their own dogs, matters were settled by dog fights.

One Sunday it was my turn to be on duty on a delightfully cool and sunny morning. I was alone whilst a KAR reserve officer was on duty in the adjoining office. It was pleasantly quiet and the corrugated iron roof of the wooden and iron building creaked as the sun warmed it and then passing clouds cooled it on that peaceful 3rd September 1939.

Suddenly Lieutenant 'Oakers' Oakrind, the orderly officer, burst in from the adjoining room. 'Government House on the phone – war declared – what do I do now?'

I explained that the War Telegram had to be dispatched forthwith and he asked me where to find it. It was locked away with the defence scheme papers in the safe and I asked if he had been entrusted with the key. He confirmed that he had, and I was able to give him the file and the telegram to send to all battalions and the Coast Defence Battery with the one code word '*Ndizi*'. This had to be sent forthwith to the Post Office and Telegraphs Department, which had been poised to ensure it received the utmost priority.

'How interesting,' he said. 'I must be off at once to tell the chaps in the mess; they will be ever so pleased.'

When he had gone I realised that in the excitement, he had not signed the telegram! Almost in a panic and without thinking I signed it myself, hoping that it would not get me into deep trouble.

However, everything went off quite smoothly. There was no trouble and subsequently I was able to congratulate myself on having taken some part in the declaration of the war in East Africa, even though nobody seemed to have noticed it. Perhaps they had all become far too busy!

There followed a time when an uneasy calm settled on the streets of Nairobi, tinged with foreboding as troops arrived from adjoining territories: South Africans, the Royal West African Frontier Force, the Rhodesian regiments and numerous others in the build-up of forces in preparation for a forthcoming offensive. The local shopkeepers took advantage of the increased population and their cash registers were kept busy.

German settlers in the previously German colony to the south, the

Tanganyika territory, mandated to the British to govern after World War I, had been expected to become a thorny menace and plans had been drawn up to round them up and intern them. Fortunately their leaders in Germany advised them that they, in their isolated position, could not expect any help from home. It would be more useful if they could get away to Germany.

Meanwhile in Kenya all able-bodied men were called up. Some went into reserved occupations such as the railway workshops which, in addition to keeping the essential railways running, found themselves having to undertake unusual jobs like making and repairing armoured cars, making land mines and other unexpected maintenance work.

Many farmers left their wives to run their very large farms and administer their labour to help feed the town, which soon became a huge garrison, swollen by troops coming in and passing through because of the large armies of the Italians on our northern frontier.

Meanwhile Miss Freda Russell travelled from England aboard the SS *Llanstephan Castle* to Kenya and very soon afterwards there was discussion on the subject of an engagement. The engagement was announced on Christmas Eve 1939, after having obtained the approval of her mother Mrs Kitty Russell. Freda and I made a pact that if I had to go into a war area we would get married right away and that on the first possible occasion I would obtain leave to do so. Then, quite unexpectedly, my unit was ordered away from Nairobi for training, and on 10th June 1940 Italy declared war against the British Empire and a new menace presented itself in Italian Somaliland to the north!

Suddenly I was given six days' leave from the railhead. This meant travelling from the railhead to Nairobi and there was not much time. Immediately I applied for permission to get married. It was granted, and my immediate superior said that, under the circumstances, they would not notice if I returned a day or so late.

Although I had managed to wireless to our new headquarters that I was coming to town, my arrival was not altogether expected at home. I managed to get home at nine o'clock in the evening. The blackout was new to me and the whole place seemed to be overhung with gloom as I walked up the path, but once indoors I found the familiar character of the old house just the same.

Freda.

When I announced my intention of getting married on Saturday there followed the most awful rush sorting things out, buying the ring, preparing the wedding reception and arranging the short honeymoon. We wanted only a quiet wedding with about a dozen friends. Unfortunately for our small house the dozen swelled to more than four dozen, but we had the most delightful reception in spite of the lack of room.

Our few friends were wonderful. My sister Phoebe worked very hard indeed, rushed round to enlist several young ladies among our acquaintances and set them to work cleaning, arranging, cutting sandwiches and so on. She also dragged my Freda all over the town getting her clothes and all sorts of other things ready.

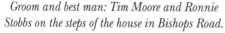

Groom and best man: Tim Moore and Ronnie Stobbs on the steps of the house in Bishops Road.

Tim and Freda wedding, 13th July 1940.

The marriage was at Nairobi Cathedral on 13th July 1940, by the Reverend Captain Jimmy Gillette (a master at the Prince of Wales School and choir master at the cathedral) followed by the honeymoon at the Brackenhurst Hotel, Limuru: all this within six days!

After I had returned to the forward area, Freda wrote a letter to her mother in England telling her:

On the Friday morning before the wedding I went with Tim to buy a ring. It is a pretty one, engraved platinum with our initials and the date inside, and we called at the bank to arrange cheque signatures. We then returned home where Phoebe was waiting to take me back to town to buy clothes. I spent a packet on a lovely white georgette evening gown, tiny buttons at back decorated with a few silver bead circles, short bolero, with elbow length sleeves and a blue hat with pink and mauve ribbons, which Phoebe took next door to have matched for a bouquet which was a lovely one of mixed sweet peas and roses, while Mrs Penfold the owner of the dress shop sent to the shop on the other side for a selection of silver shoes. I wore the pendant and long white gloves that Auntie gave me to complete the effect. I was taken to the Cathedral by Mr Moore [her new father-in-law] at 3 o'clock and the bells were ringing; I could see Tim, who seemed far away and I am quite glad Mr Moore did not walk very slowly.

Gradually there was an increasing movement of forces, including our brigade, now renumbered the 21st Brigade, towards the borders of Northern Kenya and Italian Somalia. I was disappointed when an order was issued that all European officers and other ranks north of the River Tana cease shaving. Being in the rear brigade headquarters on the south bank, we were not affected. However, I will never forget the pleasure waking in the dawn and lying in my bivouac for a few extra minutes listening to one battalion after the other, near and far, calling the reveille on its bugles.

Sometime, when we were all working hard with our heads down, a visitor blew in shouting, 'Errol has been murdered,' and some loudly responded, 'By a woman.' This was in reference to Lord Errol of the 'Happy Valley Set', whose murder was to make headlines in faraway places. We were all far too busy, though, to worry about such trivialities.

Brigade Headquarters travelled northwards in the wake of the forward troops. One evening while bivouacking on the warm banks of the River Tana, waiting for the Italians to make their threatened attack, there was a terrific explosion. Falling over the guy ropes of the office tent in the dark, the brigade major Charlton shouted, 'Moore, phone the forward company and find out what the hell is going on!' After a turn or two on the field telephone, I was answered by an old school friend, Colin Dewar, who said that an elephant had wandered in among the land mines in the no-man's-land between us and the Italians.

Although we had been on active service for some months it seemed to me to have been little more than my ordinary work carrying on

Officers' mess, 21 EA Infantry Brigade, Isiolo, 1940.

Our first camels, Habaswein, 1940.

Tim Moore, Galmagalla, 1941

under more difficult conditions, with the sounds of the elephants trumpeting in the early morning, the birds singing or a tiny unseen rodent scurrying in the grass underfoot, and above the glorious sunshine. Suddenly we were furiously engaged in the silent battle of Serenli, where we had been encamped for a while.

We became a different force calling ourselves the 29th (Phantom) Brigade. We started sending out signals repeatedly in very high-grade ciphers until I, working in the office tent, thought I would burst under the strain. The signals grew to a crescendo and then we began to make the odd mistake, so the Italians were able to break our ciphers. Gradually we took chances and began to send signals in 'clear'.

While all this was going on, Force Headquarters in Nairobi had been picking up the Italian signals, deciphering them and relaying them back to us in cipher and we soon realised that the Italians were becoming increasingly alarmed at the prospect of a flank attack from the 29th (P) Brigade. The Brigade Major was jubilant. 'They will bomb us today, or the day after,' he exclaimed and danced a jig in joyful anticipation. As we had no protection whatsoever I wondered why he was so pleased.

When the Italian bombers came over and saw our derelict trucks and a few model tanks they sheered off, as our askaris said, back to their own place. As I was a brigade clerk with my head down much of the time I did not fully comprehend what was going on but I understood that it was a feint to draw the Italians away from Jumbo on the River Juba. When they split their force to oppose the 29th (P) Brigade our advance force established a bridgehead on the way to Mogadishu.

Later, the big guns were booming and charges were sizzling over our office tent and exploding on the other side. I think it must have been at about that time I was granted my previous wish to go to the Officer Cadet Training Unit (OCTU). Before I left, the Brigade Major wished me luck and remarked, 'No doubt you will hear the Commandant's famous lecture "Blood and the Bayonet",' which was apparently his star turn at every course.

The OCTU was at Njoro, about twenty miles from Nakuru and 120 miles from Nairobi, and any cadet who was fortunate enough to possess a car could make a trip to Nairobi at weekends – to civilisation and gay music – and soon found he had many friends willing to pay for his petrol and other expenses. I would have given my all to go down and see my wife.

Njoro is a district of wide wheat lands about 6,500 feet above sea level, sloping down to the small town of Nakuru which lies at the foot of the dormant volcano of Menengai Crater. To one side of the town could be seen the grey-blue water of the lake of the same name, with pink flamingos feeding in the shallow water at the edge of the lake and the whole shore ringed with a fringe of blinding white soda. The cadets, though, did not have any opportunities to enjoy the amazing sights – pinkish clouds of flamingos rising from the surface of the water, or the waddling pelicans going about their daily business finding a living for themselves and their families. In fact few knew that flamingos build their nests up from the muddy shore on tubular mounds to provide accommodation that is easy to sit on with their long legs.

On arrival at the OCTU, each cadet was issued with a bicycle and had the gruelling experience of pedalling along rough tracks and pushing up steep grassy hills to the venue of the day's training exercise, often in pouring rain, such was the time of the year. By then the day's work had hardly begun. Packs on soaking backs were loosened and Bren guns put down while the day's instructor (who had driven up in his car or, if the terrain was too impossible, ridden on his horse) described, with what we thought was evident relish, how he was going to attack the force of 'Redland' which had bivouacked for the night over the next hill, followed by a string of ciphers which I assumed was a map reference – no good to me without a map. As they were only anything up to about ten miles away through scrub, thorns and nettles, it was necessary to be extra careful in order to preserve the advantage of surprise. It was during the long rainy season and it simply poured down all the time.

One day, while we were resting and drying our damp clothing in a burst of glorious warm sunshine, the Commandant rode up accompanied by a resplendent figure on a restless horse. He was introduced as Colonel Michael Silvester O'Rourke, Inspector General of the Palestine Gendarmerie, and explained that he had been assigned to organise and train a military gendarmerie force to police enemy territories in East Africa after occupation.

Prior to surrendering, the Italians were throwing open their extensive armouries to their indigenous regular forces known as the 'banda' or 'illaloes', suggesting that they should keep the British busy until Hitler had won the war in a few months' time, when the Italians would return. These chaps had to be rounded up, disarmed and sent to POW camps. Of course, most just disappeared into the surrounding desert with their ill-gotten booty. The desert was vast and inhospitable. Most of the people were peaceable but terrified by the 'shifta' led by merciless hostile chiefs or 'ogres' (later called 'war lords' by the Americans), and policing the area promised to be a very interesting, tough job. 'Any volunteers?'

Fed up with rain, mud, cleaning equipment, essay writing, lectures, fiddling about on the sand table and constant square bashing, I found myself in a long line of cadets waiting to have their names put down.

Strangely enough I found that the cadet occupying the next bed to mine was one of our next-door neighbours in Nairobi, a stocky Canadian, Griffiths Stephenson, with the steeliest of steel-blue eyes. He was such an enthusiast and, having been in the Kenya Regiment before hostilities began, managed to learn more about the Bren, the Boys anti-tank rifle and other armaments than some of our instructors, and so he was soon promoted to cadet under officer. His father and mother were missionaries who, among other activities, ensured that copies of the Holy Bible were placed in hotel bedrooms, labelled 'Left by the Gideons'. The missionaries conferred lasting spiritual and other cultural benefits to the many indigenous tribes whilst mastering their languages.

Stephenson, or 'Steve', who was a fluent KiSwahili linguist, was also given a language class. Our fellow cadets were from Britain, Canada, Rhodesia, South Africa and other places, and had all arrived in Nairobi. Some of these cadets had been selected by their officers to join our OCTU and for them learning a few words of the East African lingua franca became a prime objective, so Steve voluntarily ran extra classes. His pupils sat round him on his bed every evening late into the night, until he would, in his Canadian accent, say, 'Now clear off, everybody – got to study my daily piece before going to sleep!' and he would open his Bible from the Gideons.

Meanwhile British forces were approaching Mogadishu when one day we were called to parade and the names of fifteen cadets were read out and told to report to the office immediately. The parade was dismissed. The fifteen, me included, felt all eyes were on them and wondered what it was all about as they broke away from the main stream in the direction of the office.

'The Somalia Gendarmerie!'

'What the heck's that?' some exclaimed.

'You ought to know,' rasped the company sergeant major; 'you volunteered for it!'

We were to go to Nairobi that evening and buy equipment at the officers' shop next morning. Then we were to go straight down to Mombasa where a ship was waiting to take us to Mogadishu. My happy hope to see my wife was tinged with fear that it might be the last opportunity for a long time.

3

From Mogadishu to Nyasaland and Back Again

၆ၯ୷ଚ

O n the voyage from Mombasa in June 1941 the Sultan of
Zanzibar's little ship, the *Al Said*, called into Kismayu to pick up
some additional cargo. We observed several sunken ships lying on the
bottom of the harbour, left in the wake of an unfriendly visit by the
Royal Navy. We got to Mogadishu some four to five days after having
left Mombasa.

Mogadishu harbour appeared to be not much more than a jetty
built out from the shore and there were no docks at all. Our ship

Kismayu, 13th June 1941. There were six ships like this following a visit by the Royal Navy.

dropped anchor and a lighter was brought alongside to offload the troops and cargo. As the harbour was open to the vast Indian Ocean it was very rough indeed as we leaned over the deck rails watching the lighter alongside, one moment down below and in a few moments almost level with our decks, rising with a loud splash and hurling heavy spray over us.

The askaris were being lined up for disembarkation, which was effected by throwing their equipment down to a comrade on the lighter, walking down the ship's narrow landing steps and jumping on the lighter as it surged up on the heavy blue swell. Before undertaking this ocean-going experience, many of the askaris from the interior of central Africa had never before even seen the sea, and their morale was lowered by the wretched miseries of prolonged sea sickness in the hot airless hold. They just could not care any longer. They had to be cajoled, pulled and pushed up onto the deck. When the lighter rose up on the swell, they blindly threw their equipment, which on several occasions missed and sank to the bottom of the sea, whilst its owners just managed desperately to scramble aboard the lighter. Meanwhile the Sultan's good ship stank of their sour retching as brave soldiers in their misery moaned, 'Go away, bwana, leave me to die in peace.' It had to be admitted, however, that, bad and crowded as our two cabins had been, the hold below was indescribably worse and those not so affected by sea sickness were unable to get away from the presence of those who moaned and retched all over the place.

As we were driven along the palm and casuarina-lined streets of Mogadishu, several of our complement remarked that they were going to like the place as they noticed the pretty Italian girls hurrying about the streets. We were not given much time to look at the town or relax. Although I had not suffered from any sea sickness, the whole place seemed to be swaying as if I were walking on air.

We were driven straight to the 'Questura', the Italian police headquarters, where Colonel Neil Stewart, commandant of the newly formed Somalia Gendarmerie, was waiting for us to join him as he sat at the head of a huge conference table on an expansive landing on the first floor. Behind him on a pedestal was a huge bronze statue of 'Il Duce'. After we had all been introduced and exchanged a few pleasantries, he recounted an incident a day or two previously when a South African soldier, coming up the stairs, had come face to face with this statue. Without a moment's hesitation he had drawn his pistol and fired off a full chamber at it. His impulsive action, however, revealed a lack of training for, although the wall behind was spattered with lead, Mussolini still stood with massive jaw resolutely thrust forward in theatrical defiance. The Colonel said he had been anxious to have the statue removed but it weighed a ton. Anybody who could take it away could have it – but there were no takers!

Some of us were billeted in army messes but Steve and I were found accommodation in the Albergo Croce del Sud, usually referred to by the soldiers as the 'Sweaty Crotch'. We were just settling in when in the far distance a bugle called, then another, and soon it seemed as if many bugles in the town were sounding the general alarm. We rushed out, Steve following and moaning, 'Tim, I've got no ammunition.' In the excitement I shouted, 'Don't worry, follow me, I'll do the shooting!'

We were in no doubt of the direction in which we should go as many soldiers, mainly African and with fixed bayonets, rushed past us, some clad only in the shorts they must have been wearing when the alarm sounded. Gradually the crowd slowed and grew more dense as we emerged into one of the town squares where we saw Ginger Gledhill, one of our captains, parleying with some senior South African officers. We were very disappointed to find that the alarm was nothing more serious than a few drunken South Africans firing their rifles out of the window of the room in which they were enjoying a party!

Mogadishu had only recently fallen in the path of the British advance on Addis Ababa and Gonda and we were left to clean up. The population was frightened and confused and the whole place seemed to be quite lawless. Ex-Italian troops threw 'bombe a mano' about liberally, Italian houses were broken into and looted by the Somalis and many old scores were settled.

The British military occupation soon issued a number of proclamations and some form of order was quickly restored. One such proclamation was that the fascists or Italian police, officials and troops still at large should salute all British officers. It was quite unnecessary. The impact of our victory was such that even the little local children in the streets promptly sprang to attention and saluted as we passed.

Our colonel did not take long to get cracking and a visit to the prisons produced some useful recruits to his organisation.

The menu from the Albergo Croce del Sud.

'What are you in here for?' he enquired.

'I wrote a lampoon on Mussolini.' This could be confirmed as the extensive records of the fascist regime had fallen into our hands intact.

'Well, you are just the man we are wanting; you can run our local newspaper.'

Under the peaceful exterior we soon created there was a seething undercurrent. Italian men in the local underground recorded the names of citizens who cooperated with the British. Girls who talked to or even smiled at soldiers were recorded in the 'Black Book' and there was a hidden feeling of fear and intrigue. Needless to say there were strict orders to our men prohibiting fraternisation – but we could not prevent the British Tommy from smiling!

We had not been in Mogadishu long when Captain Dickey Thome called me into his office and said, 'I want you to be having a quiet drink in the Croce del Sud this evening. A cordon will have been thrown round the hotel and you will arrest all non-residents after the curfew rings.'

When the mellow bells of the Roman Catholic Cathedral, behind the ornamental palms on the opposite side of the road from the hotel, pealed out the curfew at 2100 hrs, all movement in the streets was to stop and all law-abiding citizens of Mogadishu had to be indoors while the armoured vehicles of the British occupation forces patrolled the streets. Anyone out after curfew could be shot on sight – although I must say that I never saw anybody shot for that reason.

As the last echoes of the bells faded in the darkness, I got up and went over to the manager, who was chatting to a friend in the courtyard. 'There is an armed military cordon round this hotel,' I said. 'I want your hotel register, a table and all the men and women present lined up in front of the table. I will then tick their names off in the register and any who are not residents will be arrested.'

The startled manager invited me to accompany him to his office and we went through a door off the courtyard. As we entered, he closed the door behind him and the lights went out. Quick as a flash I whipped out my revolver and stuck it into his ribs. Just then the lights came on again and there we were, I thin and alert, he elderly with my revolver stuck in his paunch. He was frightened and I, to say the least, startled. I did not know that it was customary at that time to change over the dynamo at the antiquated power station, thus causing a momentary break in the supply and instituting a convenient time check!

A stamp, a salute and an 'Excuse me, sir.'

I had almost finished ticking off the names in the register and looked up to see an enormous British soldier in the queue.

'May I have a pass to go back to my camp?'

I asked him to wait a few minutes so I could attend to him, and continued ticking off one or two more names and identities.

Suddenly, he exploded, 'Bloody hell, you keep me waiting while you attend to these bloody Italians. Don't you know they are bombing my home in Blighty?'

I asked him not to let the side down by making a fuss in front of the enemy and, at the same time, signalled to a gendarme to call the military police.

His companion pleaded with me. 'Sir, he is drunk. Please give us a pass, you would not be the first officer he has beaten up.'

I carried on anxiously aware of his menacing presence, hoping the MPs would arrive before I had to attend to him myself. Eventually a couple of burly red caps arrived.

'Sir.' The man sprang to attention, saluted and said, 'Let me have a pass now and I will go quietly.'

Fortified by the presence of the red caps, I became a disciplinarian and replied, 'No, you have had your chance.'

'I'll not go with them and I'll get you first,' he exclaimed, drawing his revolver.

The police had no difficulty seizing the revolver and disarming the drunken soldier. When I eventually went upstairs to bed I reflected that life in occupied enemy territory was not entirely uneventful!

It must have been soon after this that I was detailed to go to Nyasaland (now Malawi) to take charge of a draft of Nyasaland Chinyanja soldiers that had to be picked up at the KAR depot at Namweras near Zomba. In order to do this I had to travel via Beira in the neutral territory of Portuguese Mozambique, in the disguise of a civilian! Once back on British territory I was able to assume my real identity as a soldier.

I travelled down to Nairobi and, about an hour after arriving, was issued with a civilian passport and joined the BOAC C-class Empire flying boat at Lake Naivasha. I was pleased to find that the pilot was my brother-in-law, Captain 'Caspar' Caspareuthus, who was married to my sister Phoebe. The flight was immensely enjoyable. Caspar skilfully flew low over the plains during the flight south to view some elephants and other animals, which was something he was renowned for. We continued and landed smoothly on the waters of Beira harbour. I got a chilly shock, though, when I was told to join a line of other passengers in front of a customs officer. In near panic I caught sight of our pilot.

'Go off to the toilet,' he said, 'and I'll see if anything can be done.'

When I came out all the other passengers had been cleared and Caspar was chatting with someone at the bench. I was introduced to the gentleman, who beckoned to a customs official – 'Chalk that suitcase' – and explained that if he had opened it and found my military uniform and equipment, he would possibly have had no option but to intern me. He further explained, 'You see those ships anchored out there? They are Germans, frightened to leave because they know that a British naval frigate is out there waiting for them. Their crews and officers are all over the town and if anyone had seen that we had let a British Army officer travel through we would have been accused of non-neutral behaviour.'

That night we slept in a hotel in Beira where above the door of the dormitory wing was the command 'SILENCIO'. In the morning, after a hefty enjoyable breakfast, I caught the train to Zomba and soon I was travelling on the Trans-Zambezi Railway to Nyasaland for my appointment with the Chinyanja troops.

Having assembled the draft in early October 1941, we set off on the long journey back overland in more than a hundred motor lorries, with the ebullient Chinyanja soldiers providing hilarious entertainment. Among these soldiers was an askari, known as Private Shiringi, called by his contemporaries 'Worthless Shilling'. The trucks were driven by South African unarmed 'Cape coloureds' commanded by white officers of the South African Army.

The route took us north to Mbeya, and then we took the 'Great North Road' via Iringa and Arusha to Nairobi. There we turned right, in a north-easterly direction, to Thika and Garissa. The ferry across the Tana River took a long time, but was of interest to the troops, and then we travelled on into Somalia. It was a journey of over 2,000 miles and took the best part of three weeks.

35

'Twende safari kaskazini' ('Let us go on a journey to the north'). The convoy stops for a rest on the road near Thika, 17th October 1941.

Crossing the River Tana at Garissa, 18th October 1941.

Ferry on the River Tana at Garissa, 18th October 1941.

The long journey through the red dust was wearisome. In the evenings, when the convoy stopped, the drivers jumped out to inspect and service their vehicles before cooking their rations. However late or early, they took out their instruments and played and sang into the evening. In the morning all were off at 'sparrow fart' (first light).

When we had driven through Kenya and were approaching Kismayu in Somalia, the impish Chinyanjas were delighted to acquaint themselves with camels, which they ran along behind humorously imitating their gait. When the convoy arrived at Kismayu and the Chinyanjas got their first glimpse of the sea, they thought it was indeed a fine lake and hastened to fill their billycans with water. They found the saline tea was not to their liking.

Soon I was to leave them, but not before one of our soldiers picked up one of those pretty Italian pillar box bombs left in a previous battlefield. He tried to open it and his friend assisted by hitting it with a stick – with the result that he was put in a truck to the nearest first aid post. It was not until a long time after that I heard a cheerful voice calling, 'Jambo, bwana, remember me?' Of course I didn't until he held up his two hands with most of the fingers blown off.

Gobwen Ferry, 21st October 1941.

The Cape drivers.

Gobwen, 21st October 1941.

Gobwen, 21st October 1941.

WaKamba dance, Nziu, 29th November 1941.

WaKamba dance, Nziu, 29th November 1941.

Wajir Fort in war paint.

In November 1941 I was granted twenty-eight days leave. It can take as long as twelve days to get to Nairobi when the weather makes the roads bad, but in this case they were good and by driving at night we managed to get home in four days. My word, didn't we have to drive at high speed in some places, though?

David's birth was on the last day of my leave, on 1st December 1941. That morning a staff car came to take me back to duty and I did not see him again for a long time. John was born in more peaceful circumstances on 17th October 1943.

Meanwhile, a batch of about forty young officers had been brought out straight from England on HMS *Barham* to reinforce the build-up of the Gendarmerie force, which we were recruiting from the local Somalis and Arabs. They were briefed by the Colonel, who explained that there was a war on – as if they didn't know – and there were no raw materials or equipment. As for uniforms, he had raided the Italian ordnance stores and some recruits had to be fitted up with waiters' clothing. Hence the sentry in front of the Banca di Roma was marching up and down in a white kitchen waiter's dress shirt with a blue dicky bow. What he lacked in smartness he amply made up for in fanatical enthusiasm for the job.

Colonel Stewart explained that every possible use had to be made of local materials and the officers would have to familiarise themselves with captured arms and train their troops in their use. So these officers, straight out from the UK, not knowing a word of the local language, were expected to take over a band of half-trained, locally enlisted gendarmes and go into the hinterland. There they would continue to train their troops on the job, to keep order in their district, capture Italian troops still at large and disarm the local population.

They would be in sole charge of hundreds of square miles of territory, with their nearest British neighbour at least ninety miles away and an interpreter who knew some Italian and practically no English. Some knew a few words of that despised 'slave' language KiSwahili. The country was mostly desert, dry, harsh and inhospitable. Some got acclimatised and came to like the job.

The local population, though outwardly friendly, remembered the days when they defied the might of the British under the Mullah – known as the mad Mullah – and felt they should get themselves into as safe a position as possible before there was another change, and so disarming them was no easy task. As one old man remarked:

I have known five governments here in my lifetime. First we had a fairly peaceful time under the British, then the Mullah came, then the British came back. For a time we had the Habash [Abyssinians], then the Italians and now you have come back. Do you wonder that the only way to get a Somali's rifle from him is to kill him with it in his hand? When the Italians were running away they threw open their extensive armouries to us saying that we were to take what we wanted, keep the British busy and they would be back very soon when the Axis had won the war.

The whole country was bristling with arms and ammunition. Armed gangs of 'shifta' roamed about, terrorising the population, stealing camels from other tribes and seizing their women and children. There was dire need for law to be introduced and order to be maintained.

The Somalis are fierce, haughty nomads living in the harsh desert possibly the way Abraham may have lived. The centre of their existence is their livestock and the mainstay of their life is the camel. It has been said that the Somali is a parasite on the camel. When the water dries up, their tents, which consist of looped sticks stuck in the sand and covered with woven grass mats, are all packed up and loaded onto their camels, together with their babies and young goats, and the whole caravan sets off in search of more water. The seasonal water holes are so well known that water is almost invariably found, but along the caravan routes it is not unusual to see the skeletons of humans and their livestock.

They are composed of numerous clans, all of whom claim ancestry back to one 'Somal'. The story went that one of his sons travelled down the coast by dhow from Arabia, married a local woman and from this union developed the various clans, most claiming a unique ancestry. Each clan is a close-knit community able to trace its ancestry back to Darod, Hawiye and even Sheikh Ismail, founders of the Somali race.

They are devoutly Mohammedan and, when the day's journey is over, settle down to sing hymns and to pray. The Holy Koran, which is always reverently wrapped in a cloth, is their most cherished possession. The sheikhs, or holy men, who can speak a little Arabic and read the Koran are their leaders. Young officers of the gendarmerie were referred to as the 'infidels'.

All officers in the Somalia Gendarmerie were issued with a booklet entitled *The 'Mad Mullah', Mohammed bin Abdulla Hassan*. This man had been the dominating personality in British Somaliland from his rise in 1899 until his death in 1920. Throughout these years he had been the sole obstacle to the development and successful administration of the country. The booklet described how this remarkable man had resisted invasion of his territory by Europeans for more than twenty years and died unsubdued. The operations in 1920 are of interest in that they heralded the first operations conducted by the RAF in the role of the Empire's police. The reputation of the Mullah in resisting the might of the British Empire, among the Somalis, is the background to the present raiding, skirmishing and unrest.

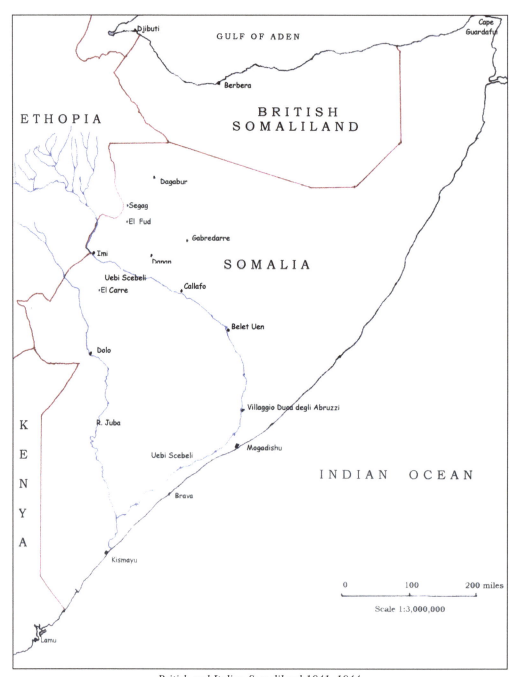

British and Italian Somaliland 1941–1944

4

On Patrol in the Ogaden, 1942 and 1943

❧

There came a time when I was ordered to Gabredarre in the Ogaden together with Lieutenants Rugg and Baimbridge. On leaving Mogadishu we drove along a magnificent Strada Imperiale, a strip of the tarmac laid along the arid sand of the desert, lightly dotted with crackling camel scrub and every few miles graced with large sculptured plaster fasces (Mussolini's bundle of sticks and an axe tied together). I contemplated this straight and smooth strategic road, which when completed was to have joined up with those in Ethiopia, eventually completing a network of roads through Somalia, the Ogaden, Ethiopia and Eritrea, past deserted wood and iron shacks, formerly administrative police or army outposts of the Italians, recently deserted and since looted by the wild, vehemently anti-Christian Somalis. Some had been reoccupied by our forces, but each of these was as much as fifty or a hundred miles from its nearest occupied neighbour.

On the journey we came to a place called Villaggio, where we found a green oasis, watered by canals from the Uebi (meaning 'river') Scebeli ('leopard') built by skilful Italian engineers. As we drove up along the approach road, shaded by mango trees on either side, Ray Mayers, the army civil affairs officer, stood up on the pleasant cool veranda of the previous Italian administrator's house and office to welcome us. Here the previous white settlers had, by their toil, made the desert bloom with grapefruit, bananas, pineapples and many other delicious fruits and vegetables. Some had remained in their old jobs on the farms and others stayed on to work the sugar mills. What a difference a few greens and water from the River Scebeli made to the whole atmosphere, and I would have liked to linger on a little longer.

Before we left, Ray asked me if I would be so kind as to drop a jeroboam of rum from the sugar mill to his friend 'Tod' at Belet Uen. When we left Belet Uen, Tod was seen busily trying to filter the rum from the broken glass and the straw in the barrel in which it had been carefully packed. I did not fancy it, and so did not remain for my share.

On arrival at Gabredarre, I was instructed to go and relieve a 'young fool' named Barnes at a place called Callafo about 250 miles north of Mogadishu. So I set off with three months' rations accompanied by Captain Gerry Hanley, which was just as well as after about twenty miles there was a big bang and our lorry turned over. There had been about twenty gendarmes and barrels of petrol and heavy stores on the open load space and, after I picked myself up from lying on top of the driver, I found that by a miracle none were hurt, but all were very excited; we had had a puncture. We had definitely been shot at by the shifta. The gendarmes called the driver a 'bloody fool', an expression they had picked up from the British troops. Fortunately, Gerry was able to let us have one of his lorries and we were able to continue, he now going off in a different direction.

On arrival at Callafo, I was shown around by Barnes, who proudly informed me that he had been transferred to the British Military Mission to Ethiopia. I anxiously enquired how he was to leave. 'On foot?'

'Oh, no,' he replied, 'I will have to leave by motor lorry.'

'Where is your lorry?'

'I have never had a lorry. I'm to go in the one you came in. Here you have to move everywhere on foot.'

As I watched from the prominent veranda of the previous administrator's uncompleted bungalow, I saw my erstwhile vehicle shrink to a pinpoint heading the long spearhead of dust on the plain below and I felt a remote loneliness welling up around me.

The uncompleted Italian administrative post consisted of two partly built houses, abandoned at the outbreak of war, on a prominence surrounded by the Somali village. The only room capable of being locked had been strengthened and utilised as the armoury. It contained possibly 150 Italian carbines, a few Breda machine guns, several boxes of 'bombe a mano' and a shotgun and revolver exquisitely chased, the woodstock delicately inlaid with mother of

Callafo.

pearl. During Barnes' raids to disarm the local people, these had been taken off the most prominent Somali chief, the Ugas Olol Dinle, who had received them from the Italian government after the Italo-Abyssinian War in appreciation of his services in leading up to 10,000 shifta against the local Habash (Abyssinians), who were then in occupation of the Ogaden. Thereafter, the Italians had annexed the Ogaden to Somalia. Subsequently the British military occupation designated it a 'Reserved Area' with ownership and status to be decided after the cessation of hostilities.

With reluctant curiosity, I took out my map to ascertain the lie of the land. I was about eighty miles from my nearest European neighbour at Belet Uen, about ninety miles from my Ogaden commanding officer at Gabredarre, approximately 140 miles north-west to Imi, which was held and administered by Lieutenant Iain McDowell (later awarded the Military Cross), while Captain Ray Mayers had recently set up a post at El Carre, about 150 miles due west.

My study of the map was interrupted by Sergeant Kituri, my second in command, a former Tanganyika policeman. I was pleased to have him in my unit because here was somebody I could understand, who spoke KiSwahili. The rest of my two platoons, one Arab and the other Somali, besides their own languages knew some Italian, and a smattering of that 'slave language' KiSwahili. The Somalis regarded their southern neighbours in Kenya as inferior people with woolly hair. Anyone with a tendency to grow woolly hair would spend much

47

of his time combing it out. Briefly, I gave orders for PT at 0700 hrs, parade, inspection and drill at 0900 hrs, small arms and bayonet practice before lunch, and guard mounting and 'tamaam' parade in the evening, along with posting of sentries, a vital necessity.

At night, I could not bring myself to lie down in either of the shells of the two uncompleted bungalows. When I shone my torch through the doors I was almost enveloped in flights of startled bats trying to escape the light. They swished past me, eerily almost caressing my head.

As I lay on my camp bed under the gorgeous starlit sky, I fell asleep hearing the villagers below chanting the Koran and singing Mohammedan hymns. Soon I awoke to the sound of the Mufti calling the faithful to prayer, the crowing of many cockerels, the dogs, the goats, the women and their babies and the whole village becoming vibrant with sounds of life of a new day.

It was not long before I felt I had been there for ages, sending selected men out on patrols, north, east, south and west, and leading some patrols myself, leaving the brave Sergeant Kituri to look after the base and the ammunition store, whilst always pursuing the shifta and endeavouring to disarm as many as possible. On return, there was the routine checking of the arms and ammunition.

Our rations arrived at irregular monthly intervals by motor lorry or occasionally by camel, when the roads were flooded by the rise of the River Scebeli. Before anything could be done I had to go through the mail, official letters turfed onto one side and those from my wife eagerly opened and read straight away. Due to the erratic deliveries, there was often more than one. The arrival of the rations was as eagerly anticipated by the men who were anxious to receive their cigarette rations, without which they 'could not go out on patrols and fight'. From my vantage point on the hillock on which the house was built, any dust cloud miles and miles away in the arid plain below could be observed, and as it grew and grew – surely it couldn't be anything other than our rations, and so the excitement intensified. It was amusing to watch my wonderful Sergeant Kituri checking the rations with one of our rather raw recruits, who was handing articles down from the lorry. He would pick up such items as a couple of toilet rolls and, after a keen inspection, exclaim, 'Two books!'

The little hillock was visible from many miles away and, returning

'Tim Moore on Patrol in Somalia', a cartoon by Gordon Drysdale.

from patrols, I used to look through the simmering heat mirage to see if I could see the Union flag still flying. Seeing the flag still flying was an indication that the station had not been raided nor the armoury broken into by the shifta.

It was my job to maintain order over a vast tract of country, sending out patrols, fighting and disarming the shifta and continuing to train my gendarmes. As previously described, just prior to their capitulation in the town of Mogadishu, the Italians had thrown open their fully stocked armouries to Somalis exclaiming, 'Harass the British and we will be back in three months, after the war in Europe has been won.'

49

At first, the prestige of the victory was so high that we had no difficulty in disarming our earliest contacts, but gradually the bulk of the illicit arms went underground, only to reappear on the frequent camel raids or to settle old scores. Consequently, it became necessary to organise some local intelligence and follow up all possible leads. After the visit of an informer, a section of gendarmes was sent to the rer (a Somali desert tent) to arrest the owner and confiscate the weapon.

I had to train my men, some of whom were newly enlisted, in such things as parade ground drill, weaponry and bush warfare. I instinctively felt they knew more about the last than I did. They certainly had a better instinct for finding their way in the desert, especially at night when there were few stars and we were in a bowl with a smooth horizon all round – no church steeples or poplars or bushy-topped trees! I soon also found out that in bayonet training it was quite unwise to pair off a Somali and an Arab. I had to separate men amongst whom there were feelings of racial antipathy.

Meanwhile, reports of trouble used to come in from almost every direction – shifta brigandage, inter-clan feuds, camel raids and murders. So, unable to be everywhere at once, I used to send out small patrols, say a corporal and ten men, in different directions, almost beseeching them to remember their training, exercising the utmost vigilance and posting sentries while taking a rest or at night. All went quite well and they would come back with fair reports and occasionally captured arms, until one day a gendarme came back alone. A notable shifta bandit named Serad Alikasse, for whom they had been told to look out, and his cohorts had come across them in the night (he had possibly been observing them during the day), shot and killed six men and got away with their rifles.

I had to report this incident to headquarters. We had signal pads with which to write the reports, and these were sent initially by runner to Belet Uen and then onwards by their regular motor lorries to Mogadishu. It must have taken some time, but I soon got a message that our commandant, Colonel P R Mundy, 4th KAR was coming to visit me. Hastily, I got trusty Sergeant Yusuf to summon a parade and I instructed the men to turn out in their smartest uniforms to salute and present arms. As mentioned, my house, office and armoury were at the top of the hill and the guardroom at the bottom at the driveway leading up to it.

David Drayton and Colonel Mundy, DSO, OBE, MC.

The Colonel approved of our turnout and some new barrack accommodation and latrines which I had had built. 'Can't have them going anywhere, all sorts of illnesses.' That evening we sat down to a sundowner and evening meal on my veranda during which he insisted on his own bottle – he had a better supply. I had only got a little Dietz lantern and he grumbled about the miserable gloom. Meanwhile his servant set up his sleeping accommodation and I wondered what the morning would bring forth.

In the cool sunny morning, his cook, as efficient as all colonels' cooks I supposed should be, produced the breakfast. When I asked what the Colonel proposed for the day he briskly replied, 'Can't stay here any longer, must be away,' and he added sternly, 'Now, look here, my lad, I don't want to hear of you getting any more of your men killed. Remember, if they find that they can kill your men, they will think they can kill you. They may kill you, and if they find they can kill you, they may try to kill me – and that's where I draw the line! You must frequently march out in strength, show the flag and hold field firing and bombing exercises. Good morning and good luck.'

So away he went in a cloud of dust in his field car, leaving me completely squashed. However, I cheered up when, a few days later, a motor vehicle arrived with, among other things, a beautiful Coleman pressure lamp. So I now felt he must have had some goodwill and his impression of me was not so bad after all. (I had been a brigade clerk when he commanded the 4th Battalion KAR at Bombo, Uganda.)

I used to go out day after day in between occasional days in camp, drill and routine matters such as paying the men, making out lengthy acquaintance rolls and answering headquarters bumf.

I had been told, 'The only way you can get a Somali's rifle from him is to kill him.' I soon saw the only way to get arms and ammunition was to allow my men to string a captured suspect up on a tree with his elbows tied behind his back (a torturous position) in the blistering sun, occasionally beating and haranguing him. Meanwhile, we sheltered ourselves in any shade we could find until he confessed where he had hidden his arms or until we found he could hardly be broken down and must be innocent after all.

Another more subtle method devised by Lieutenant Taylor, a big Scot who always wore a kilt and a huge Scottish regimental badge in his cap even miles from anywhere, was to round up a number of suspects for questioning at night in a lonely deserted rer.

'Now you must tell me where your arms and ammunition are or I will have to shoot you. No? It's your last chance. Sergeant Abdi, take him out and shoot him.' There came a loud bang and a low moan in the outer darkness and the hefty Tubby continued, 'Now, who's next?' Then, 'Abdi, bring in that man you shot.'

I was not there at the time and, although it could have worked the first time, I doubt if it could be used again!

Next time I met Tubby he was commanding his platoon on a fine horse and he was becoming rather a legend among the people on his district. Needless to say, I think the horse was enemy property which he sequestered!

Anyway, I decided I must shut out any squeamish feelings and become insensitive to extreme measures against gangsters taking pot shots at us. Moreover, there were often problems with casualties. My men received skilled attention from the Italian medical clinic when necessary. The shifta nearly always managed to recover their wounded, but on one occasion we did capture a wounded shifta. A debate arose as to what to do with him, miles from any shelter, and although we managed eventually to get him to Callafo, he lay on the ground fearlessly eyeing us whilst one officer even felt like shooting him because he had just recently been trying to kill us.

On a hot and sultry day, a message was received by runner from headquarters in Gabredarre ordering me to occupy an ex-Italian fortress at Danan, about eighty miles north, and we did so after a long march. My word, was I tired! My men had been used to such long walks since the days of their childhood with their parents, always searching for muddy water holes in the desert.

The fort had an irregular stone perimeter with a circular wall at each corner, which allowed both sides to be covered by defensive fire. The fort was made of nice big stones the like of which I had not seen before in the dry sandy desert, probably having been brought in by transport. It was enclosed by a many-stranded circle of barbed wire. Outside the main entrance was a burial ground, desecrated by the local hostile tribesmen. A little further outside lay the remains of a crashed aeroplane.

I had hardly got in when I was visited by a Colonel Collingwood, who admired my watercolour sketch but criticised the use of too much green. He was appalled by the violation of the Italian soldiers' graves, left since the Italo-Abyssinian War, and instructed me to make the locals re-bury the bones and tidy the place up. Then he went away and left me with a problem. The local Somalis, many of them gangsters and some embryo 'war lords', did not think it at all wrong to profane 'galkas' (infidels). I summoned their chiefs and ordered them to do what was necessary, and they agreed 'if the inferior people are not allowed to look on.' A machine gun proved to be a good persuader.

Inside the perimeter were the buildings evacuated by the Italian soldiers, and I inspected the office and sleeping quarters and hoisted the Union flag. Then followed days of idleness. I felt lonely and bored and wondered why I had been sent there as I went through the daily rounds, infantry training, firing machine guns, throwing 'bombe a mano' about and endless office work.

I was delighted, however, to receive a visit by Lieutenant Charles Winnington-Ingram, a relative of the Bishop of London, which made quite a nice break from the routine. A Somali also presented me with a baby cheetah. It was ever so playful and never seemed to rest by day or night, which presented problems, one of the least of which was its frightened objection to the soldiers stamping their feet when they

Painting of Danan Fort.

Painting of Danan Fort in the distance.

Baby cheetah, Danan, 1942.

Illalo sergeant, interpreter Mohamed, Tim with baby cheetah and Ali.

saluted or came to attention. It was perhaps because the fort was walled all round that it did not escape, although I had no doubt that it could have done so. Perhaps it was because it was still only a kitten.

Later came Brigadier Scupham, who roundly scolded me for flying the Union Jack at half mast. It was the Italian flagpole and I had no means of climbing up and repairing it. Anyway he did not wish to stay any longer in such a godforsaken place and off he went, leaving me in solitude with my ragged soldiers and baby cheetah.

On my return to Callafo (I do not know why on earth I had been sent to Danan), morale among my men was low. The surrounding country was lawless and bands of vicious shifta from the borders of the Habash (Abyssinia) carried out marauding raids into the Ogaden. The main raiders were from the lawless Rer Abdille, Rer Amaden, Rer Abdallah and Rer Telemughe. The venue of their operations was from the Ethiopian border eastwards to El Fud and then southwards down to the Callafo area, crossing the Uebi Scebeli to seize livestock from the people in the settled areas.

These swift raids were often on a considerable scale, carrying off hundreds of camels. Sometimes women and children were taken back with the shifta into the highlands on the other side of the Ethiopian border, all on foot, so fleet that they could hardly be intercepted.

Danan, November 1942.

Danan, Christmas 1942.

Many of the raids across the Uebi Scebeli could only be made when the water was shallow. When the heavy rains came to the highlands of Ethiopia, heavy floods poured down the Uebi Scebeli and its surrounds and the non-Somali riverine peoples were able to sow their seeds of millet and other crops. Until the country dried out, communication between Callafo and Mogadishu was not possible, except by camel through to Belet Uen. We had no radios.

The Ubei Scebeli, which flows 1,547 miles from the highlands of Ethiopia to the Indian Ocean at Kismayu. It is the fifth longest river in Africa.

Tribesmen sympathetic to the shifta kept them informed of movements of Gendarmerie detachments, and efforts to contact the shifta were disheartening. They were so mobile, driving their booty at great speed, but gradually we were being given more motor transport and better arms. Even so, the best way to ambush the roving brigands was by foot patrols. It was easy for them to detect motor vehicles from their dust trails and their noise.

Moreover, one vehicle I used continually dug itself into the sand, where it got very hot and stalled. On such occasions, the driver would loudly shout, 'Ha-fuff!' and off we would go. Being curious, the second time it happened I went round the back and saw a man jump off. He cupped his mouth round the petrol tank pipe, took a large breath and blew with all his strength a hefty '*ha*', ending with an exhausted '*fuff*', and away we went. Having satisfied my curiosity, I took no further notice until one day, after a '*ha-fuff*', burning petrol came out of the engine on which I was resting my arm. My clothes were burnt and the men managed to beat out the flames. Of course, I had to be taken down to the hospital in Mogadishu. I was not admitted but treated as an out-patient.

Quite soon I was back in command and sent out scouts to find out as much as possible about the various gangs of raiders who terrorised the local people. One day I was visited by Colonel Llewellen – 'Long Lou'. I do not remember whence he came or where he went, but he caused a sensation among the people who came from miles around to meet him. He lived on meat and camel's milk and was thought to be the only white man thoroughly fluent in the difficult Somali language. He told me not to bother with trying to sort out their various clans. He knew much more about them than they did themselves. They gathered around him in large groups wherever he went to listen to his stories.

Still the camel raids went on. The shifta plundered, murdered and stole livestock, goats, women and children, with the camels being very useful in carrying their loads and driving their livestock booty back to their lairs.

Rer Ugas Nur (Rer Abdille) dance to celebrate election of Mohamed Abdi Yassin As Ugas, 1942.

Rer Ugas Nur (Rer Abdille) dance to celebrate election of Mohamed Abdi Yassin As Ugas, 1942.

No.1 N.W. Prov.   S E C R E T.   OPERATION ORDER NO.2

REF. MAP *BELET UEN 1/1000,000*   COPY NO.

                                                       5th October, 1942.

INFORMATION.

(a) The following signal has been received from Headquarters
    "Operations start tenth Oct against SHIFTA in area north Kenya Bdy.
    "All Ethiopian bdy south Webi Scebelli incl Taylor and tps El Carre
    "coming under comd RITCHIE. One pl CALLAFO proceed immediately
    "route march in force (?reinforce) El Carre. Taylor with one platoon
    "patrol southwards from El Carre to contact platoon patrolling
    "North from FILTU. All posts on frontier North El Carre furnish
    "patrol (? patrols) and to exercise vigilance."

(b) Capt. Paton Ker has been placed under comd. Gendarmerie for these
    operations, if fit, but it is believed that this officer may be sick.

(c) Lt. Cooper is sick at Gab. & Capt. Wood temporarily i/c Dagabhur,
        Dagamedo and Sagag.

(d) Gendarmerie must NOT cross the Ethopian border.

(e) Rains have broken and may delay movement by M.T.

INTENTION.

(a) To give effect to the H.Q. orders given above.

(b) To locate Gen. FRANCES CHINI or FRANCESHINI and his party and kill
    or capture them if in Somalia territory.

METHOD.

(a) Lt. Rankin to Dagamedo leaving Gab. 5th Oct. To meet Capt. Wood,
    take over from him command of "D" Coy. (Sagag and Dagamedo) and
    arrange scheme of patrols and intelligence.

(b) 2/Lt. Virgin to take over command of "B" Coy. Gab. from Lt. Rankin.

(c) O.C. Prov. to move Danan and thence take 2/Lt. Moore to Callafo to
    organise move of platoon to El Carre.

ADMIN.

(a) Lorries Nos. 77 and 130 have been made available by S.P.O.   They
    will be returned to Gab. at earliest.
(b) Lorry parties to carry 7 days rations.
(c) Platoon from Callafo to El Carre to take 28 days rations by A/T.
    Patrols normally to take 28 days by A/T.

INTERCOMM.

    Information regarding (a) Shifta (b) Italians to Prov. H.Q. and
    nearest P.O. by fastest means.

ACKNOWLEDGE.

                                                        Major.
0900 hrs.   O.C., N.W. Province.

Distribution.

O.C., El Carre.   O.C., Dagamedo
O.C., Callafo.   O.C., Dagabhur.
O.C., Danan.   O.C., Prov.
O.C., Sagag.   P.O. Dagabhur   ) For
                          A.P.O. El Carre) information.

5

The Ambush: Operations Against the Shifta on the Uebi Scebeli

❧❦❧

It was on 12th January 1944 (for once my diary was precise), when I was back in Callafo and about to go for a gallop on Del Rey, the beautiful horse once belonging to the Mayor of Mogadishu, that I had a message from Lieutenant Colonel Collingwood. He had received news of a large party of shifta from Lieutenant George Todd in Gabredarre, it having been signalled from Segag, near Gololcha on the Ethiopian border. It appeared nothing immediate could be done and, in fact, I did not record in my scribbled diary where Lieutenant Colonel Collingwood was at the time.

On 13th January a message was received from Lieutenant Carpenter at Imi that there was lots of trouble and shooting from shifta gunmen prowling round his camp. 'For Christ's sake, what can be done?' Lieutenant Colonel Collingwood, often coming and going at the time, was furious about the 'panic', but he, of course, was not in the lonely isolated outpost. At 1500 hrs, my corporal Abdi Farah returned from patrol with two prisoners and two rather old rifles which he had captured.

I should have been collaborating with Lieutenant Bruce Minnis, with his two lorries and thirty gendarmes, but he was always on the move and without any radiotelegraphy we might easily have been going in circles round each other. Bruce, the Merchant Taylors' schoolboy, used to tell me that he believed in kneecapping bandits who it was reliably alleged had concealed arms. True or not, he was a stern character who had earned the sobriquet 'Minnis the Menace'.

Reports of the gangsters' movements were as usual very confused –

each poised to steal from and kill his neighbour. So it was in the early morning on Saturday 15th January, after stand down, that a party of the Rer Mgab came into our hidden bivouac and complained that they had been raided by a party of more than 200 Rer Abdille or Rer Amaden, armed with rifles and a Breda LMG. They said it was about two days ago, so I decided to wait a while longer and hoped to get into contact with Bruce Minnis. Goodness knew where he could be in this large open country. Bruce was always on the move and camp would be where he had bivouacked the previous night. Possibly he had gone on to Danan or Segag. He was an indefatigable walker.

It was on January 16th that I again received reports from different bush telegraph sources of elusive shifta at Farar and Melka Taka. So we proceeded in the two trucks which I had somehow acquired and, on arrival at Melka Taka, sent the lorries away and forded the river crossing. We heard the sound of a gunshot and got excited. However, it turned out to be no more than a couple of my illaloes who were trying to attract my attention – strange ways those irregular scouts had.

In the hot midday, the dusty mirage rose, blotting out the landscape all round. The bush in the foreground is covered by the fine dust during operations in January 1944.

On Monday 17th January, I decided to halve my platoon and load up the lorries and drive again to Melka Taka. Raiders would have to cross the river in order to get their booty back to the protection of the 'shag': the unfamiliar scrublands of the Habash (Abyssinian) border. So I decided to choose a spot which had not been used recently, to sit down and possibly be lucky for a change. I had just settled down for a quiet read when, at about 1700 hrs, an exhausted runner from the elusive Bruce Minnis said he had seen shifta approaching Degahale. Very light gangs, but I concluded it was stale news.

Meanwhile, I just kept my men on the river bank hidden in the scrub, trying to read and wave off a persistent fly buzzing round my face, a bloody nuisance in the torrid heat.

On Thursday 20th January there was more movement of detachments than I had previously seen. Bill Ryan, captain of the Mounted Infantry squadron of the Gendarmerie, arrived with two lorries carrying new P40 (.303) rifles to replace the captured Italian .256mm carbines on which my men had been depending and also one of the new, at least to me, Sten guns with which I later tried to shoot the guinea fowl resting in flocks under the scrub, sheltering from the midday sun. I never managed to hit anything with it. Moreover, it was a dangerous light-triggered weapon, likely to release a stream of lead on the least shake. Can't remember if it had a safety lock! Later a Major Whalley and Captain Fyfe passed with their detachments of the Somaliland Camel Corps. Since they were motorised I wondered where they had left their mounts!

After they had gone, on January 21st, I decided to leave Melka Taka with twenty-five gendarmes, two Breda LMGs, the newly acquired Sten gun, three large metal boxes of .303mm cartridges, sixteen boxes of .256mms for the Bredas, nine barrels of spare petrol and full tanks. We also took rations for the troops, none for me as, when on patrol, being lazy, I just ate the same as my men. It was a change from the time of my first arrival at Callafo when I seemed to have nothing!

We got away at about 0930 hrs and arrived at Baadlei at about 1230 hrs, having left the motor vehicles under guard and walked several miles. We paused on the riverbank, having sent two scouts west to Kerker and another to Birale. We did not take a lorry as the shifta scouts would see our tyre marks and conclude they were fresh, as otherwise the wind would have covered them in the soft powdery sand.

The patrol from Baadlei brought back two Mgab men who said that Rer Amadan and a few Rer Adan Khier, numbering about one hundred in all (fifty men and fifty boys), had seized their camels at Adadle the previous day and were expected to return any time.

Two Gadsir Dir reported that their camels had been seized at Gerri, near Bur Eghi, by Rer Abdille with twenty-six rifles and four unarmed men. They thought the gang would have crossed the river at Helawagah or Birale. They also reported that Rer Abdille tribesmen observed our positions on the river and carried the intelligence back to the shifta.

At about 1800 hrs, we heard voices and stood to, but it was only one of our scouts. He brought in three Rer Afgab and one Rer Gadsen from Ber Waren, who reported that the shifta had raided and seized about 700 of their camels at about 0600 hrs: a sad loss to people who live off the backs of their camels. I very much doubted their figure, but they insisted and maintained that the marauders' strength was about one hundred men with many rifles. Soon after that, tribal scouts said they had seen a motor lorry pass with a few men who they thought were gendarmes of the Mounted Infantry squadron as the men were wearing turbans. The lorry stopped and someone on it waved, and they went off again before the scouts could get to it. All this added to my general confusion as to what was going on.

After discussion with other chaps, whom I was beginning to meet more often, I decided the best way to bump into the raiders, who after their murderous raids invariably slunk back into Ethiopia, was to wait for them in ambush. No good trying to catch them on foot. They were more fleet of foot and knew the country better. The terrain did not lend itself to the use of motorised units.

Accordingly, after several 'reccies', I got a hunch on January 22nd that they would as likely as not cross the river at a suitable spot such as Baadlei and decided to settle down there, hidden under the shady branches of the trees which grew along the moist banks of the river. These trees gave us some protection from the unbearable heat of the midday sun. The first task was to obliterate any signs of a possible ambush from the keen eyes of the enemy, and so my men were sent back along our approach and returned gently patting out our footprints in the soft sandy soil approaching our position.

Then we lay under cover of the trees and scrub and waited and waited and waited, ate our meagre rations, talked and dozed. Meanwhile one of the troop, called 'Nairobi' by the rest of the men (because they thought his name 'Banubi' sounded like 'Nairobi' – but not so to me!), stealthily followed a bird along the banks which he uncannily knew would lead to a beehive, where he stole some honey – which was ever so welcome and a refreshing change to our rations.

Local riverines (a non-Somali, Bantu people) kept us at a pitch of excitement, reporting that a very large party of Rer Amaden shifta raiders was approaching the river with many stolen camels. The problem was where they would be likely to cross. Surely we would not be waiting so tensely for nothing?

On Saturday 22nd January, a signal was received by runner.

To Moore or Minnis, No. 2/2 of 21 Jan. from Fife, SCC ... stop ... Information from Barry & Corfe ... stop ... Large body of raiders with camels expected to cross at points east of here possibly Rarunley ... stop ... Will put post on crossing here and patrol your way first light 22nd Jan ... stop ...

This was received at 0700 hrs and I jotted a hasty reply on my message pad, carried back by runner:

My No. 1 of 22nd Jan. ... stop ... Your 2/2 ack. Located at Boranlau ... Indications are that large armed party up to one hundred, repeat one hundred will cross today or tomorrow if no M.T. or troops seen ... stop ... Will watch here ... stop ... Suggest no M.T. be used in vicinity ... Quite able to cope ... stop ...

I paid the runner one shilling, quite good money in those times.

At about 0715 hrs, hearing voices, the platoon was alerted, all stood to and nine men of the Rer Garden clan arrived. They had seen the shifta and they were 'coming this way': about 150 men and 'thousands' of camels, the desert dust of which could be seen in the distance and getting nearer.

0915 hrs.   Three motor lorries under command of a Somali sergeant of the Somaliland Camel Corps arrived – an unwelcome interruption, likely to spoil our ambush, so I sent them back to Helawagah.

1000 hrs.   Scouts reported raiders assembling stock – as always camels.

1010 hrs.   Three lorries – apparently our force – were seen behind our front travelling west, but in the 'fog of war' we did as usual wonder who they were and what they were up to.

1040 hrs.   Aulihan tribesmen acting as our scouts reported that a party of shifta fired four rounds in their direction while they were drinking, I believe, on our side of the river. The scouts reported six were with rifles.

1100 hrs.   Waiting in position, strict silence, suppressed excitement.

1200 hrs.   Gendarmerie reported voices, camel noises. Heard nothing myself; perhaps their hearing was much more sensitive.

1210 hrs.   Shifta, driving camels across the river right in front of our position, being much interfered with by their rightful Aulihan owners.

1220 hrs.   Sergeant Yusuf let off a round and for a few seconds our disciplined silence was broken by all hell of gunfire. The enemy fled and I ordered my men to get after them. One was seen lying on his back on the opposite side, his hands held up in supplication as perhaps he prayed. As my men (Mohammedan brothers) passed, some stamped their army boots on his upturned face. At that stage I had only one man wounded and four shifta killed.

1330 hrs.   It was quiet and, as the fine dust settled, blotting out the bright sun and spreading a gloom, as oft-times happens in the hot desert, and we were chasing the scattered enemy, firearm reports everywhere, I felt an intense loneliness being the only white and Christian. I found myself praying, 'Father dear, let me not perish in a place such as this.'

Sergeant Gurrach MM, with captured camels after the battle at Baadlei, 22nd January 1944.

The recaptured stock taking water in the Ubei Scebeli at Baadlei, 22nd January 1944.

Then, as if in answer to my prayer, there rose a great excitement among my men, who were laughing and cheering, 'Lorry, lorry.'

To attract their attention we detonated three Italian 'bombe a mano'. When they emerged out of the warm mirage, I was happy to see sun-tanned white officers. Soon a Captain Widdecombe jumped out of the leading truck followed by our commandant Colonel P R Mundy, DSO, OBE, MC, Captain Macdonald, Lieutenants Holdhurst and Davidovich and Sergeant Cross, the last of whom I had never met before. The Commandant expressed his pleasure of the operation which had resulted in the capture of 800 camels and five shifta confirmed killed, with many others killed and wounded carried away by the shifta, out of a force of seventy-five, at the cost of one gendarme slightly wounded. After mugs of tea, he left us, handing charge of the greatly enlarged force over to Captain Macdonald and his two squadrons of the Somaliland Camel Corps.

I was given no scope and they would not allow me to take out a few gendarmes to see if there were any more dead, in the scrub or as indicated by vultures, spiralling and no doubt descending. He seemed to foresee the possibility of a counter-attack or sniping during the night. Nobody was to venture beyond the perimeter and anyone wanting more than a gentle relief would have to 'bake it until the morning'. All I could foresee were lurking shifta trying to steal the odd camel on the fringe of the very great herd we had recaptured.

Operations against the shifta on the Uebi Scebeli continued and, between 23rd January and 26th January, other Gendarmerie units stopped several bands of raiders and recaptured camels at several different crossing points. As a result of these actions, the shifta were becoming demoralised and were splitting into small parties. Captain Ryan and his mounted infantry had also pursued and captured many bands of raiders, and by 30th January reports suggested that the shifta had become completely disorganised. The report of these operations, which is reproduced in Appendix I, shows that some 2,000 camels were recaptured and thirty shifta either killed, wounded or captured.

The foregoing is a sample of what we had been doing, and had to go on doing, during our long, wearying military occupation and government of the captured Italian colonies of Somalia and the Ogaden.

Mounted Infantry squadron, commanded by Captain Bill Ryan, leaving Callafo.

It was after I had been at Callafo for about eighteen months that I was given leave to go down to Nairobi. I was to be relieved by a young Rhodesian Army Rifles officer, Lieutenant Fisher, who was serving in the Gendarmerie. Our paths must have crossed as I left for Mogadishu and he for Callafo at about the same time. Alas, when I returned from my leave I found that the station had been raided by the shifta, the armoury broken into, and he and some other gendarmes had been killed. So I never met him.

The ferry over River Juba at Bardina.

Quartermaster's stores, Forte Checce, 1944.

Sgt Yusef and one gendarme with oryx shot near Melka Taka, 1944. It made a welcome change from army rations!

Wajir Fort restored to former glory.

The Lido at Mogadishu. Painting by B A Sopra, 1944.

Mogadishu, 1944.

Mogadishu, 1944.

Harvest festival, Mogadishu, 1944: black bull leads and is regarded as fertility symbol.

Harvest festival, Mogadishu, 1944: crowd following the above photo. Reggie Cater, MC, looking on.

Ancient mosque in Mogadishu, mentioned by Vasco da Gama in his despatches to Europe.

Mogadishu, 1944.

74

At the end of my service in Somalia and the Ogaden on 30th July 1944, and although I was anxious to go, I did feel regretful in leaving Callafo, where I had made many friends among the peaceful resident Somalis and Arabs.

Unfortunately I became ill with a severe kidney infection and was sent to the tented army hospital in Nairobi for some weeks. Afterwards, I was put on light duties to continue my peacetime activities as a captain on the staff of the 2nd Echelon and Military Records Department in Nairobi.

The occupied enemy territory administration by the British Army carried on until the defeat of the forces of the Axis, but before then I had left sunny Somalia.

In February 1946 Bruce Minnis, Army Civil Affairs Officer, Duhun, Ogaden Province, Somalia, wrote in a letter that 'There is no raiding or trouble of any sort at the moment'.

V J Day parade, Delamere (Jomo Kenyatta) Avenue, Nairobi.

Captain S J (Tim) Moore, V J Day.

Military Records, Nairobi (Tim Moore sixth from left, front row, and Major Dewar eighth from left).

Freda, Morris Eight and Mount Longonot in the Rift Valley.

A trumpeter of the band of the 3rd Battalion, King's African Rifles. During the war the band's instruments were sent to the bank for safe-keeping. The bandsmen were given other duties such as stretcher bearing etc.

Part 2

PREFACE TO PART 2

❦

When my father died in 2002 we found the first five chapters of this book which had been typed up in draft form, together with some notes on further material and some photographs. My brother and I gathered all this material up together with some additional boxes of photographs and papers and cleared his flat for sale. All this material lay dormant for a while until such time as I was able to go through it and sort it out.

My father had been a good watercolour artist and did some nice paintings, and from this he became interested in photography and became a keen amateur photographer and enjoyed developing and enlarging his films. Wherever we lived he converted the garage into a dark room. There he would spend evenings with his chemicals for developing and fixing in various dishes, and with his enlarging camera he produced many fine pictures. Fortunately some of his paintings and photographs survived all the moves and they were amongst the boxes we cleared from his flat. Some of these are now in this book.

We also found two diaries, one of which, 'The Somalia War Diaries', was used for the preceding chapters. The other one, of 1946 to 1949, provided the material for the next chapter. There were also many letters, miscellaneous orders, reports and lists of equipment from the time he was in Somalia.

The final chapter owes its existence to a file of 'Probation Service Bulletins' that the first principal probation officer asked his secretary to keep. The next principal wanted to throw these away, but these papers were liberated by my father! This chapter is supplemented by the many letters received from his friend Pius Oloo, which kept him in touch with the developments in Kenya and the Probation Service for many years after he left.

I would like to acknowledge the help I have been given in checking and proofreading all the text by Dr Annette Rose and Kenneth Rose, and John Rose's help with the photographs. This work could not have been completed without the help and encouragement of my wife Carolyn, daughter Louise and son Robert. My thanks go to all of them.

D R Moore
Poole, Dorset

6

Home Leave

❦

On Wednesday 20th March 1946, the wide main platform of Nairobi station was crowded with travellers who were boarding the waiting Kenya Uganda Railway's train bound for Mombasa, together with a large number of those who wished to see them off and to wish them 'Bon voyage!' Two days previously we had assembled at the transit camp to attend a briefing at 'Z' Company and to change some money into English currency.

Freda and the two children boarded the train and settled into a carriage with a Mrs Howison and her two children, while I was to travel separately in an ambulance carriage, which was very comfortable. Everybody seemed to be there, with many friends and colleagues all wanting to say their farewells. The locomotive whistled as we left and a party of other ranks on the platform could be heard singing 'Auld Lang Syne' whilst the band added to the general pandemonium.

As we drew out of the station on our 330-mile journey to the coast we passed the goods marshalling yard full of wagons, then the engine shed with all the locomotives gathered round as if contemplating the next duty roster. All the tracks beside ours gradually reduced till, finally, the line to Nanyuki swung away to the left and we were on the single line to the coast. The sprawl of Nairobi disappeared and we were travelling over the rolling wide Athi Plains dotted with thorn trees and where giraffe, zebra and many other animals could be seen. In the distance the Ngong Hills gradually grew smaller and smaller till we could no longer see them. I spent the afternoon in the family carriage. Next morning, we arrived in Mombasa at about 0745 hrs and, after waiting about an hour in a siding, we went on to the quayside in Kilindini harbour. We boarded the troopship *Cameronia* at about 1000 hrs and had breakfast.

The Ngong Hills.

*

Friday 22nd March 1946. All day long the boat filled up with a great variety of passengers. All shore leave was stopped and that was a very good sign. There was a continuous hubbub of conversation everywhere and this did not make it any easier to hear the frequent announcements and orders over the loudspeakers. Freda and the two boys were in a four-berth cabin with another woman and two children.

It was announced that just before the ship sailed there would be a 'stand to' at boat stations at about 1545 hrs. Whilst we were 'standing to' the ship started to move. After that we were given the signal to cease boat drill and I went along to see how Freda had fared. John, who was two years old, was fascinated by the locomotives on the docks shunting backwards and forwards. Our departure seemed to have created quite an excitement in Mombasa, with people lining the sea front waving and tooting on their motor horns. At the harbour exit a couple of naval boats sounded their sirens. On board, the loudspeakers announced that the seas were still heavily mined and instructed everyone to take boat drill seriously!

After a week at sea there was a very badly organised baby show. After the show the speakers requested the mother of 'No. B3' to call at the Naval Regulating Office, where we learned that young John had won third prize in his class. The prize giving was at 1645 hrs and he was given some sweets, toilet soap and a packet of 'Rinso' – very unromantic but useful articles.

David and John developed a passion for climbing over the donkey engines, railings and up ladders. One day a sailor stopped and asked me, 'Have the nippers been up to the crow's nest yet?'

It was announced that we would be picking up Italian prisoners of war at Port Said and proceeding thence to Naples to disembark them. Strict instructions were issued in regard to fraternisation and it was threatened that those who disobeyed would be disembarked at Naples – if they were still fit after the sentry had arrested them! I judged that we were well into the Red Sea and the heat, though probably not as torrid as later in the year, was still oppressive.

Later, I was detailed to pay RASC, RAMC, RE and NAAFI-EFI personnel. There was a fixed scale: warrant officers were allowed 30/- (£1.50), sergeants and above 20/- (£1), and below sergeant 10/- (50p).

*

Saturday 30th March 1946. Officer commanding troops issued an order that all Navy, Army and RAF personnel would wear uniform from tomorrow morning until the ship sailed from Port Said. If this rule was not strictly observed the privilege of wearing plain clothes for recreation and sunbathing after luncheon would be withdrawn.

The weather became pleasantly cool below decks. On deck it was chilly in the breeze but very warm in sheltered sunny alcoves. Housey-housey was a favourite game on the aft promenade deck and there was also a 'race meeting' up there in the evenings, but we did not attend.

The next morning it was distinctly chilly but we found it pleasant to sit in the sun on the aft promenade deck. This opinion appeared to be unanimous, judging from the multitude, and the place was rather crowded. We were just in time to see the *Athlone Castle* gracefully pass within a stone's throw of our vessel with her lavender hull, gleaming white superstructure and black-topped red funnel. This made a vivid change from all the uniform wartime grey of most other shipping.

The day was one continuous changing panorama. Unfortunately, we dropped anchor at Suez during luncheon and so missed some interesting sights. When we came up we were in time to see the vessel which brought our oil tie up, and 'bum boats' arrive optimistically trying to sell their wares.

*

2nd April 1946. When we left they said we would have 'boat stations' every day, but they relaxed this order somewhat and it became obligatory for Italian PoWs only. I was officer for the day and went round on inspection with OC troops, the captain and other ship's officers. It was very interesting to visit spacious, cleanly swept decks, NCOs coming smartly to attention, kit arranged neatly in the overhead racks and neatly piled hammocks visible in the gloomy corners. When the vessel had been converted to a troop carrier, what had obviously been holds for cargo had had tables and racks for hammocks installed. Extra ventilation shafts and electric suction pumps had been fitted and the area was lit both day and night by electric light. Quite a few not quite so obvious other modifications must have been made, such as extra water tanks – even though water was strictly rationed – and installation of extra cooking facilities.

We observed the PoWs at their midday meal. This consisted of a most appetising-looking gruel, the palatable aroma from which reminded me that our luncheon time was drawing near.

There was a concert in the evening called 'Homeward Bound' which Freda and I enjoyed despite the cold. We bought some Turkish delight and sugared almonds at the canteen. These had been taken aboard at Port Said. David took the trip in and at Port Suez he told a passenger, 'There is a big ship outside and it is giving us some oil. It came from Port Suez' – not bad for a four-year-old! The last duty at night was to see that everyone had vacated the public rooms so that the staff could clean up by 2300 hrs.

When we woke up the next morning we were thrilled by the sight of the beautiful snow-covered mountains of Crete suspended over the horizon like delicate feathery clouds.

I had to pay the personnel again on the day after that and the paymaster said he hoped this would be the last pay day of the voyage, unless the 1,400 troops we were picking up at Naples required any money. We hoped they would have been paid prior to embarkation.

A faint coastline emerged out of the mist at about 1500 hrs, with cold, snow-covered mountains appearing to be suspended over the misty water. Later, as we cruised into the Straits of Messina, we passed Mount Etna on our port side – an exquisite delicate misty subdued blue, wearing a feather of smoke. The whole scene resembled a picture from a fairy storybook, as the watery setting sun picked out pink and white buildings in the misty atmosphere. Whilst watching this panorama from the promenade deck, John, who was rather lively, amused the Italians below. He was not slow to notice this audience and was soon showing off every trick in his small repertoire. He had to be removed lest his antics should result in his falling down a companionway or over the railings. The Italians obviously love children!

*

Friday 5th April 1946. 'La belle Napoli,' uttered one PoW as I went to the fore deck in the morning and saw what looked like a fairy castle rising out of the mist. We finally tied up about 0830 hrs, and soon after that the Italian prisoners of war began to disembark. At first the battered quayside was quite deserted except for some British military police and a few Italian port officials. After a little while some members of what looked like a very scratch brass band, in drab civilian clothes, began to assemble. There were no wives, no sweethearts, not even a civilian spectator to greet these returning soldiers. Our bows were facing inland, stern to sea. On our starboard was the celebrated Vesuvius and on our port a corresponding lower hillside feature clustered with pink, white and cream villas surmounted with what looked like a castle or walled monastery. All this rose out of the pale blue mist suspended over the oily calm harbour waters.

There was a great deal of shipping in the harbour. On our left, flying the stars and stripes, was the *William Brewster*, a Liberty ship, the newest vessel in harbour. In comparison, others were drab and patched, some were being painted with red lead paint, and others were still lying where they had been hit. Staging had been built over one sunken vessel beside the quay, extending the edge to its outside bows so that the dock could again be used. This was presumably done in haste. One vessel showed successive rings round her hull suggesting that she had probably lain on her side and been raised to a horizontal position by degrees. A barge with a crane on board was carrying debris about for disposal, probably by dumping it out at sea.

There was no shore leave for all at first, though the crew and permanent staff were later allowed off. The 'Old Man' gave me permission to disembark long enough to photograph the ship. Shabby Italians furtively tendered watches, silk stockings, ladies' underwear, trinkets and cameras. These were not for sale for cash but in exchange for cigarettes for onward sale on the black market. Our table steward had managed to get a watch, which he let me have for what he paid for it or possibly plus a little profit, so I gratefully paid him 300 cigarettes.

Quite a number of aircraft flew over the bay and a trim, fast Italian naval vessel left and returned in the afternoon. She left again in the evening and we wondered what mission a gunboat of a defeated nation could be undertaking.

The next day we left Naples. Whilst we were breakfasting, the Italian naval ship, which must have returned during the night, speedily overtook us and was soon lost in the misty morning drizzle.

The following is a brief summary of the *Cameronia*'s war record:

Sep 39–Nov 40	Passengers & war material between Glasgow & USA
Jan 41	Converted to troopship
Mar 41	Landings in Greece
May 41	Evacuation of Crete
Nov 42	Landings in N. Africa
Dec 42	Torpedoed – reached port and repaired
Jun 43	Landings Sicily
Jun 44	Landings Normandy (largest troopship present)
Aug 44	Landings S. France

Survived 44 air and/or submarine attacks, and credited with destruction by gunfire of one Heinkel III and two Junkers 88.

Transported 400,000 troops to the invasions of North Africa, Sicily and Normandy (*Cameronia* was the largest troopship that took part in June 1944).

The crew were awarded:

1	CBE (Capt. G B Kelly)
5	OBEs
2	MBEs
10	BEMs

It is noticed that this ship, the *Cameronia*, was built in 1921, by Wm Beardmore, Dalmuir, for the Anchor Line for service on the North Atlantic from Glasgow to Liverpool and thence to New York.

*

Wednesday 10th April 1946. This morning I stood in a queue until 11.30 to get a haircut. Then the barber came out and announced that he was closing at 12.00 and so I saw no further use waiting and my hair remained uncut!

When I went on deck, the first thing I noticed was that Freda was standing up looking rather miserable. This was rather unusual as we are usually sitting on the blanket at about this time. Freda was frozen! Both boys composed a touching picture, lying soundly asleep on the deck with only silky flaxen heads peeping out of the green blanket.

Methodical preparations, such as issuing of landing cards and division of troops into drafts for various destinations, reminded us that the pleasant journey was nearing its end. Clouds obscured the morning's pleasant sunshine and it was distinctly chilly.

It was amusing to note that when the speaker on the wireless system made an announcement, whether long or short, he always terminated it, 'That's all.' When we were about to pass Mount Etna, he volunteered the information, 'The only continuously active volcano left, which erupts once every minute. That's all.'

The great game of the day was to identify and then correctly challenge a mystery passenger – 'Labby Lug'. Anyone possessing a 6d ticket who successfully completed the challenge received £1. The younger passengers actively pursued clues.

*

Friday 12th April 1946. The weather was very cold on deck and the children preferred it below; they formed long snaky 'trains'. It was most amusing to watch them choo-chooing up and down the corridors, each 'carriage' occasionally letting out its own independent shrill whistle. The 'train' was a serious inconvenience to adult passengers passing along these corridors and a danger to stewards carrying buckets, jugs, plates or trays. The wireless greatly supplemented their childish shrieks. John, the smallest, was a most enthusiastic unit of rolling stock.

We missed Dublin Bay but upon enquiring why there was the most cacophonic howling noise coming from the bathroom. Someone said it was the BORs (British Other Ranks) singing because they had seen a distant coastline, which could be none other than that of old Blighty. There was an impromptu dance in the first-class lounge.

Next morning at about 0530 hrs I rose and went up for a shave. The vessel was quiet and appeared to be motionless. When I looked through the bathroom porthole I saw for the first time the banks of the Clyde fringed with picturesque houses in a cool grey that harmonised with the morning mists.

'Yes, we are back again,' they said. 'Look at that Scotch mist, it is the genuine article, known here as the real MacKay!'

But the mist gave promise of a fine day and, as the cool but bright spring air touched the hills and the banks, it seemed to me, seeing them for the first time, they outrivalled the Straits of Messina through which we had recently passed.

We passed the magnificent *Queen Elizabeth* being refitted for her peacetime duties. The panorama of the rising sun revealed her true grace but, due to the dense crowd jostling me against the railings, I was too late getting my camera into action. We passed a battle-scarred Union-Castle liner being returned to civilian use. David and John were wide-eyed, not at the exquisite beauty of the scene, but at the wonderful ships and exciting machinery they saw.

Many civilian passengers had sent radiograms to travel bureaus endeavouring to book accommodation in Glasgow, but they got negative results. This was because the great international football match was on that afternoon and 'Glasgie' was already, as we afterwards discovered, overcrowded. Even at this stage we soon found Glasgow was thinking of nothing else but the match.

As we drew alongside the deserted wharf, the first two gentlemen to greet the vessel were two MPs, and the troops let out a good-natured but nevertheless thunderous 'BOO!' Before we had tied up, the speakers started to broadcast continuous and confusing instructions and all became organised chaos. When nightfall arrived, it was difficult to realise that about 3,000 troops had been disembarked and numerous civilians attended to by the ship's crew. The main sufferers were the crew whom we all forgot to thank, tip and bid goodbye before leaving in such a bustle and bewilderment.

We caught the train at the docks platform at 1225 hrs and here again we found we had not got rid of the loudspeakers as an unnoticed loudspeaker suddenly issued instructions. Previously in the day, I had been to the Bellahouston Transit Camp, where I had lunch, obtained some documentation and noticed speakers were employed there also.

It was a very cold, uncomfortable overnight trip on an overcrowded train to London's Euston station, where we were met next morning by Freda's mother and her aunt. Together we all travelled to Colchester. The weather was gorgeous, the cuckoos calling and the whole countryside a spring garden. First impression was one of 'normality' and not the disorganisation we had expected. The date of our arrival was 14th April 1946.

*

The victory celebrations took place in London on 8th June 1946 with 21,000 troops from Britain, the British Commonwealth, Empire and allies, following the end of World War II. They consisted of a military parade through London, with the flag bearers of most of the allies who took part in the war (except the USSR, Yugoslavia and Poland due to the Cold War). More motorised military units and marching columns and bands followed. After sunset the important buildings were floodlit and King George VI, Queen Elizabeth and their family were carried down the River Thames in a barge, and the day ended with a fireworks display.

The band of the King's African Rifles had performed in Edinburgh before the London parade. Hyde Park was used as a camp site where troops from all the Commonwealth and Empire congregated.

*

21st June 1946. I had to return to Kenya, having completed the job I had to do in England. I bade farewell to Freda and the boys, who could not come with me, and travelled to London and then to Liverpool where I was met by Margie, my sister, and her husband Dickie, who were living there. After taking my luggage on board the SS *Antenor*, I managed to get some leave and went to dinner with them. Dickie came back to the boat with me and we drank some beer, which we had managed to smuggle aboard.

The next day, before departure, General W A Dimoline, CB, CMG, CBE, DSO, MC, Commander-in-Chief, East Africa Command, came aboard to say goodbye to the East African Victory Contingent. As we sailed from Liverpool a British band played on the dockside. Whilst we drew away the King's African Rifles band on board played 'Auld Lang Syne'. I watched as Dickie's figure on the dockside grew smaller and smaller.

Liverpool had seemed a straggling, very extensive and grimy city on first superficial acquaintance, with few open spaces. The feature which most impressed the askaris was the Mersey Tunnel. The citizens whom I saw appeared tired and shabby and, judging from the large percentage of worn clothes, seemed to be mostly workers or dockers.

My cabin companions were:
F/Lt McClure, 'Shawn', RAF
Capt. John Wrightwick, Suffolk Regt
Capt. Bill Williams, REME
Capt. Shields

Maj. Bromley, Lt. Home and other 'Cameronians' were also on board. Among the East African contingent were Stephenson, Basil Pickering, Weary Wood, Powerie and Charlie Broomfield.

Five days later we were cruising under cloudless azure skies when we passed Gibraltar, the outline of which was softened by the wispy mist rising out of the glassy blue sea. The motion of the propeller could be felt all over this ship, which had been used by Blue Funnel Line on their far eastern services before being called up for war duty. She had also served as a troopship in Operation Overlord in Normandy in June 1944.

*

1st July 1946. Arrived at Port Said in the early morning. As my job that day was orderly officer, I had to go round the ship asking hawkers for their passes and handing those who had none to the Egyptian police with the threat that any who returned would be put into the ship's guard room. In between time I amused myself trying to take pictures of traders who had climbed up the masts of their feluccas in order to get nearer to buyers on the higher decks. We drew anchor at about 1600 hrs and entered the Suez Canal.

*

0025 hrs, 2nd July 1946. I had just settled down to get some sleep in the orderly room when the phone buzzed and the executive officer, Major Noble, requested me to tell the people playing the gramophone on the top deck to stop it and go to bed. Shawn McClure, Lt Rueben (in pyjamas) and one lady were in the party, which I had to interrupt.

At Port Suez, at the southern end of the Suez Canal, a number of South African troops embarked.

*

7th July 1946. Arrived in Aden, where there was a very strong gale and sandstorm blowing, to disembark a passenger with appendicitis. However, we were unable to leave that evening owing to the gale, which blew the vessel towards the shore on casting off so that there was danger of wrecking the jetty from which the ship had just drawn oil. It took two tugs several hours to push the ship back to a buoy to be tied up till the storm abated.

The ship departed Aden next morning, passing the *Empress of Australia* whilst having breakfast. There was a strong rumour among the passengers that a hurricane was blowing in the Indian Ocean. Later orders were issued that all hammocks and loose kit on troop decks had to be made secure and so we went round tightening up on decks etc. and closing portholes. 'Chinstraps' (John Wrightwick) spent most of the day polishing his boots, Sam Browne etc. acting as usual.

*

13th July 1946. Our sixth wedding anniversary. Hope Freda received the message from Cable & Wireless and liked it. The ship anchored outside Mombasa in the evening.

The ship arrived at Kilindini harbour, Mombasa, early next morning and tied up at the quay. We boarded the troop train for Nairobi. However, all passenger trains for up-country had to go via the main or upper level station in Mombasa, where there was the usual public address system which directed us to collect NAAFI comforts: sandwiches and one bottle of beer each. Needless to say we bought very much more beer for the journey and we departed at 1730 hrs. It was a very slow train as it did not arrive in Nairobi until 1500 hrs the next day and so most of the day was spent drinking beer, while John 'Chinstraps' polished his boots yet again. As the train approached Nairobi, in the haste to get ready for disembarkation, a glass of beer accidentally spilt on to Chinstraps' shining results.

My dad was on the station and also CSM Frost with a car from Records. I went along to Records and met Watson, who said I was to work with him.

*

Due to the shortage of shipping following the war, it was not until February or March 1947 that Freda, David and John, together with Mrs Russell, were able to return to Kenya sailing from Southampton aboard the RMMV *Winchester Castle*. In the immediate post-war period even the Union-Castle Line's Cape Mail ships, which had survived the war, were used on the East Africa service. In due course after a very pleasant voyage the ship arrived in Mombasa.

However, the train journey from Mombasa to Nairobi was more eventful because the train broke down and made very slow progress. Instead of passing the halfway point of Mtito Andei station in the middle of the night, the party found themselves in the dining car having breakfast there! A replacement locomotive was summoned to take the train onwards, which turned out to be one of the KUR's impressive EA-class locomotives. Although less powerful than a Garratt it had a reputation for fast running. Thereafter, the journey progressed in fine style and the countryside, normally passed in darkness, was revealed in daylight. David and John had their heads out of the window most of the way to Nairobi.

UNION-CASTLE LINE.   R.M.M.V. "WINCHESTER CASTLE."   20,012 TONS.

Winchester Castle was built in 1930 by Harland & Wolff, Belfast, and rebuilt in 1938 with more powerful engines and single funnel. During the war she served as an assault training ship and troopship, and took part in the Madagascar, North Africa, Southern France, Sicily and Anzio landings.

"28" CLASS LOCOMOTIVE

KUR's EA class (reclassified 28 class by EAR), built in 1928 by Robert Stephenson & Co Ltd, Darlington, was for many years the principal locomotive type for passenger trains on the main Mombasa to Nairobi rail section.

In later years, when new ships came into service, the sea route was the preferred method of taking 'home leave' (or 'DOMCOL' in the Army). Shipping companies like Union-Castle, BI and others tried very hard to make the journey to Europe as pleasant and enjoyable as possible, and the new ships being introduced from 1950 onwards all had air conditioning to make the passage through the Red Sea more comfortable. In addition the merits of a sea voyage with nearly a month's 'free food and rent', but possibly a large bar bill, were much more attractive than the four days' expensive travel in the flying boat and then finding accommodation in the UK for an extra three weeks.

When BOAC introduced the modern Constellation and Argonaut airliners, with pressurised cabins, quicker journey times and economic fares, flying became more attractive. However, it was the jet airliner, together with containerisation, which brought an end to the wonderful sea voyages that were enjoyed by all. Sadly, the style, grace and beauty of those lavender-hulled Union-Castle Line ships are gone forever.[1]

---

[1] The 1951 Belfast-built *Kenya Castle* was one of the last survivors. She was converted to a cruise ship in 1967 for the Chandris Line as SS *Amerikanis*, and went for scrap in 2001.

7

Post-War Life

❦

After about four years in the bush and desert I had become too unsettled to resume my pre-war work with records in the 2nd Echelon, in charge of quite a number of ATS. I applied for a more active job and was posted to the Kenya Immigration Department which, at that time, came under the jurisdiction of the Kenya police. This job offered much more satisfaction involving tracing illegal immigrants and sending them back to where they came from. Pressures from the Gulf States between Kenya and Arabia and the long coastline presented enormous problems in keeping out Indian and Arab would-be settlers or immigrants.

The department had had a long history stretching back to the previous century when British gunboats captured and then released human cargoes from Arab dhows all along the east coast. The Arab slave trade, supplied by the Kabaka of Buganda by the sale of his people in exchange for rifles, is well chronicled in *An Introduction to the History of East Africa* by Marsh and Kingsnorth (CUP). I have an appreciatory book in KiSwahili, *Uhuru wa Watumwa* ('the freeing of the slaves') by James Mbotela, whose grandson became well known to me when we worked together in the resident magistrates' court in Nakuru. We spent many happy hours practising our KiSwahili while Freda made tea for us on our sunny veranda.

Meanwhile, the routine task of checking the airline passengers off the incoming flights at both Lake Naivasha (where the Short Solent flying boats landed) and Eastleigh airport on the outskirts of Nairobi (for normal aircraft) was carried out. Sometimes, I used to take David with me to Lake Naivasha. We travelled in the BOAC buses, which were Bedford lorries made up with crude angular wooden bodies, and when in the hands of their African drivers these lorries showed a remarkable turn of speed. The journey was about fifty miles along a road recently improved and laid with tarmac by Italian prisoners of war. This involved the ascent to the top of the Kikuyu escarpment. From here there were magnificent views into the Great Rift Valley with the extinct volcanoes, with Mount Longonot and Mount Suswa easily visible. The descent down the escarpment could be magnificent and hair-raising at the same time before progressing to the lake in the valley floor. David seemed to enjoy the journeys. It was amusing to watch him pointing out the animals en route, or trying to calm down more nervous passengers who did not appreciate the 'skills' of the drivers. BOAC ended flying boat operations with the Short Solent flying boats in 1950.

Flights into Eastleigh airport could sometimes bring long delays and if any overdue aircraft was coming from England, via Entebbe, it would not be expected until late at night. I then used to go home and listen for its arrival. It was fortunate that we lived near that flight path as we did not have a telephone in those days. On hearing an aircraft which sounded like the one expected, I would jump into the car and drive to the airport in time to check the weary passengers.

Flying boat City of York on Lake Naivasha.

Occasionally, if it was very late, the street lights would be switched off to save on imported fuel for the generators; the Tana River hydroelectric schemes were some years in the future. The Milky Way and the stars would be gloriously bright in the thin air due to the altitude at which Nairobi stood.

After a few years in the Immigration Department, I saw an advertisement in the government circulars calling for applicants to join a proposed new Kenya probation service. I was not initially interested. However, shortly after that I met up with my old acquaintance David Dewar. When I had volunteered for the Somalia Gendarmerie, he had volunteered for the British Military Mission to Ethiopia. He had been mentioned in despatches, had been decorated by the Emperor of Ethiopia with the order of the Lion of Judah, and had risen to the rank of major. He said to me, 'Why not join me in a good job in which you may find you are doing some humanitarian good?'

Colin S Owen, a probation officer in the United Kingdom Home Office, had just been sent to be the first principal probation officer for

Avro York at Eastleigh airport, Nairobi. These planes regularly flew over our house.

Government Road after World War II.

Delamere Avenue after World War II.

Kenya. There were volunteers among the Kenya police and the United Kingdom police and probation service, as well as some local residents, out of whom Colin Owen was able to form his small service. He selected Major Dewar as his senior probation officer and second in command: a very sound move as Colin, knowing the law and court procedures, did not know how to set up an office or have any knowledge of local languages and customs. So I joined the Kenya probation service and became a probation officer in Nairobi.

Masai, Kikuyu, Jaluo and other tribes soon got a desire for European wares and were welcomed by enterprising Indian traders. The tall 'warrior' is bargaining for a 'shuka' or sarong, whilst his woman in the beads faces the camera. The packing case bears the legend 'Made in England'. The Shell Petrol Guide to the People and Animals of Africa records that there are forty different tribes speaking forty different dialects in Kenya – hence the growing popularity of KiSwahili.

Masai 'warrior'.

The M'Kamba curio seller, August 1951. He sells hand-carved figures in wood.

*A passenger train in 1949–1951 approaches, climbing out of Nairobi, as a
Kikuyu woman carries her load uphill.*

*A 58-class locomotive (introduced in 1949) and train pass Kikuyu settlements west of Nairobi, with
the outline of Ol Donyo Sabuk in the background.*

A Kikuyu boy herding cattle and sheep watches the photographer with interest as the train, with the coaches in the pre-1948 brown and the short-lived cream livery of the newly formed EAR, heads up-country towards Kibera.

Meanwhile, symptoms of hostile unrest in the Kikuyu tribe gradually increased. I had known, even before the war in my clerical intelligence work, of the political agitation and later of the indescribably filthy Mau Mau oaths decent men were forced to take, losing all their self-respect. So much so that they would obey any order to commit murder. Most were simple and uneducated, but others with some education and Christianity became informers and cooperated with the government.

Although most of the African tribes longed for the time when their country would become self-governing, they remained for the most part patiently law-abiding, with the exception of the Kikuyu, who were much the largest, most powerful and most impatient group. The situation was simply fearful and there were murders of many Africans and a few European settlers, including wives and children. There was a daring raid on the Naivasha police station by terrorists down from the Kinangop in the Aberdare Mountains using, for the most part, their own handmade guns. I used to see the police armourer testing such weapons, made from old tubing, elastic and stolen live rounds, but I never saw one go off.

In 1951 there was a call from Mr Rodwell and Miss Rugg-Gunn (the resident magistrates in Nakuru) for a probation officer to be based at Nakuru. The principal probation officer (Colin Owen) said to me, 'This was started by Mr Gillespie and Mr Goudie (earlier resident magistrates) and has been going on long enough; house or no house, office or no office, you must make arrangements to go to Nakuru and take on a few cases.'

Hence I arrived in Nakuru on 7th January 1952 as the probation officer for the Rift Valley Province and before the end of the year one hundred persons had been placed on probation.

The first offender to be released after having been convicted of taking the Mau Mau oath at Nakuru was placed on probation on 27th February 1952 and sent to the African Inland Mission at Kijabe. He completed his probationary period on 26th July 1954 and was employed by a firm of building contractors.

Karanja, the man who I believe was the first surrendered gangster to be treated – the forerunner of others – was released on probation on 22nd January 1954. I took him to the Kabazi canning factory and asked them to risk employing him. Later I paid a visit and was told by the factory manager that Karanja was in sole charge of a machine and was one of his best employees. When I asked Karanja how he was getting on, he said he was doing well but had a serious complaint. Whenever the bwana wanted him he shouted, 'Where's that terrorist?' I reported this matter to the factory manager and an amicable settlement was soon reached!

Nakuru town is located just below the bulk of the extinct volcano of Menengai Crater, which, although rising only 1,500 feet above the town and surrounding country, is massive. It has one of the biggest calderas in the world at 2,000 feet in depth and a diameter of about eight miles. With regard to housing and office accommodation, we stayed for three months at a hotel called the Prairie Inn about four miles out of town. After that we rented a bungalow with a sunny veranda, which was just at the start of the rising land below Menengai Crater and had a lovely panoramic view westwards of the Mau escarpment to the front, with Lake Nakuru and Lion Hill visible to the left.

However, this part of the Rift Valley was suffering from the effects of a drought which was to last two years and Lake Nakuru was strongly affected. The lake was usually replenished with water that had run

The Prairie Inn, Nakuru, where we stayed for three months.

over volcanic soil and contained minerals from the lava. With no natural outflow, evaporation in the heat concentrated these minerals and salts, which made it a soda lake and gave a white rim to the blue waters of the lake. It was this soda, containing so many minerals, which promoted the growth of algae on which the flamingos fed.

As the drought went on, the rivers which fed the lake dried up and the evaporation continued. The area of the lake decreased, showing less blue water and more white rim, resulting in an increase in the salinity. The flamingos which were usually there in large numbers, being unable to feed, flew away to other soda lakes in the Great Rift Valley. Eventually, the lake dried up completely until it was pure white. In the heat of the day the dusty surface heated up and began to rise up in the atmosphere, only to fall back again as night-time temperatures dropped. As the drought wore on and it got hotter and hotter, the soda dust cloud started rising earlier and earlier in the day. If the wind blew it in our direction it was awful, stinging our eyes and burning our throats. It was like driving in a London smog. We were always relieved when it blew in another direction.

Eventually, the rains did return and it was a lovely sight to see the clouds rolling down Menengai as if they were a giant steam roller intent on flattening everything in its path, bringing the rain to settle the dust. After a while, when the lake began to fill up, the flamingos did return. Just a few to begin with, but then it seemed every day more and more flew in and circled the lake, as if to make sure that the rumours were true, till eventually the lake had all its pink flamingos. The pelicans and other migrating birds all returned. Only then could we see the spectacle of the shifting mass of pink moving over the blue waters of the lake as millions of flamingos fed on the algae.

Office accommodation was soon obtained, just a stone building with three or four small offices and a large general office with a waiting area. Gradually a band of assistant probation officers and office staff was built up and, although from different tribes, they became a very good team.

Often, when I was attending court in the old wood and iron court house, the corrugated iron roof 'clonked' as the sun went behind

The daily second- and third-class all-stations passenger train from Nairobi to Nakuru and Kisumu, with the now-standard EAR livery of brown and cream, stands at Kikuyu station with the 29-class locomotive taking water, about 1954. This train took seven hours to reach Nakuru and fifteen hours to Kisumu on the shore of Lake Victoria. Some may find it hard to accept that this peaceful scene was taking place in Kikuyu land during the Mau Mau emergency!

a cloud. The doors creaked and the dry twigs and seeds of the blue gum trees could be heard tinkling on the corrugated iron roof. The magistrate thought he could hear something else, and he hoped it was the woodworms or something else that caused rot and decay. Whatever it was, he wished that it would speed up its work. After all, it was time that the town got a new court house. The building was so old and rotten that when, out of spite or contempt for the law or merely to destroy a file, someone tried to burn it down, it would not ignite.

The peace of the moment was destroyed by a scuffle and a huge, scantily-clad Masai man with a red-ochred pigtail was pulled and pushed into the dock. The magistrate directed the interpreter to read the charge out to the accused. The giant, staring out of the door in aloof detachment, became aware of the little court clerk. Cupping the palm of his hand behind his ear, he bent down towards the object that had attracted his attention and grunted, 'Huh?' The court clerk repeated himself and the giant raised his voice. '*Huh?*' The court clerk tried once again and the giant raised his voice again. '*HUH?*'

The court clerk turned to the magistrate. 'Accused pleads guilty, Your Honour.'

The accused was put on probation and stalked along after me, with his blanket flapping, as I walked to my office. I explained that as he had stolen Major Brown's greatcoat whilst in his employ as a herdsman, he was now on probation and would have to report for the next two years.

When the wearisome and tedious formalities had been completed I, his guide and philosopher, asked my newfound friend where he would be spending the night. He indignantly replied, 'At Bwana Lordi's' (Lord Hamilton, who was much esteemed by the Masai). He added that he would like a note to go to a local rural police station to collect his greatcoat.

'But you cannot have the greatcoat,' I replied. 'It has to go back to Major Brown.'

'Oh, well, in that case can I have a letter to collect my deposit?'

Completely bewildered, I gave my wild friend a letter for the police station asking them to make the necessary investigation.

The matter was almost forgotten until a few days later a huge figure was seen to come riding perilously down the hill on a bicycle, bare buttocks revealed as his greatcoat was blown up behind. As he passed me he waved merrily and greeted me with 'Jambo, bwana!'

It was a pleasantly exhilarating job. The government ordered the army and the Kenya police to round up Kikuyu troublemakers and confine them in internment camps in several different parts of the country. It fell to me and my African assistant probation officers to visit camps in a Kenyan police aeroplane, covering much of the country, with a view to discovering any detainees who might be suitable or repentant enough for release on very strict probation. We would then return them to ordinary life and employment under supervision of the very good team of loyal African assistant probation officers.

In the Probation Service Bulletin No. 2 issued in February 1956, the principal probation officer and chief inspector of approved schools, Mr Colin S Owen, wrote, 'After many years' endeavour, the amendment to the Probation of Offenders Ordinance has at last been passed by the legislative Council. African Courts can now be given the power to use Probation Orders in suitable cases. This will be done in the first instance by selecting suitable African Courts and these will appear in the Official Gazette.'

In April 1956 the Nyando African court, in the Nyanza Province, was the first African court gazetted to start using the probation service. An assistant probation officer was appointed and, starting without a house, office or transport facilities, made such good progress in the cases taken on. This experiment was deemed to be successful and, later in the same year, it was decided to gazette eight other African courts, from the Coast, Central, Rift Valley and Nyanza provinces, to start using the probation system. This achievement was the result of years of hard work and came at a time when the emergency was receding and the service was better equipped to meet the extra demands, at the start of the second decade of the probation service of Kenya.

While all this was going on, Freda could not see so many people working to rescue the country without offering to lend a hand. So I had a talk with 'Monkey' Johnson, the senior provincial officer in Nakuru, and soon she was offered a position as a secretary in the provincial office and became almost an indispensable member of staff. (Why 'Monkey' we do not know. It was said he was so called even by his wife, although he was normally good-looking.)

Pius Oloo, on the left, presenting the cup.

I feel I must include a note about my great friend, who sadly I fear must have passed away since I lost touch with him: Pius Nicholas Jacob Owea Oloo (to include his various names), who joined me as an assistant probation officer. He had no hesitation in speaking in the courts and Mr Justice Goudy said, 'He is one of the Africans who have got the Europeans summed up.' He was the secretary of the Luo Football Committee. He was very black and to see him riding off on his motorbike with David, then so blond, on the pillion behind was most amusing.

Pius was later transferred to Thomson's Falls, which is on the Laikipia Plateau and is nearly 8,000 feet above sea level. He was a great letter writer and wrote:

Regarding Thomson's Falls, there is nothing constructive and of interest that I can tell you. All I can say is that the work seems to be getting on well although I do not find the climatical conditions congenial to my health and the family and as such I am not quite satisfied but there is nothing I can do about it, as it is a matter which is above my dealings. I am sorry that I have to mention about discontention of this place every time I write, but it is because you are the only one I could trouble. May I have your advice whether it would be worthwhile putting in an application for a transfer or whether it would be wise to be quiet for some time, but I am so worried that I may have to lose one of my children due to such unusual weather conditions of this place.

Pius eventually got a promotion to Kakamega, which was much more to his liking.

*

In early 1958, we had to say goodbye to Nakuru and to the many friends we had made over the years and move back to Nairobi. This was in preparation for a handover from my old friend and to take over the position of senior probation officer.

On 31st May 1958, Major Dewar retired with thirty years in the service of the Kenyan government (plus many years serving in the Army), of which a third was in the probation service. His work was a good example of patience, tolerance and endurance. It was a valuable period for the probation system, and he brought a strong conviction that it was right and worthwhile. He had no doubts about the remedial value of probation as a means for treatment of offenders. He had an enthusiastic approach to the 'chance' in life and often took a chance to save a man from going down for a stretch.

One of the other duties that fell to a senior probation officer was to represent the Kenya probation service elsewhere, and soon afterwards I attended a conference in Uganda. I heard workers from almost every territory in Africa tell us what they were doing. It soon became apparent to me that, possibly apart from South Africa, the probation service of no other territory had achieved anything like the standard set by Kenya and none was as progressive. For all this, the credit is due to Mr Owen, who arrived in Kenya on 9th November 1945 and, from being a lone worker in the courts of law, built the service up to its present standard.

Not only was the service started on a shoestring but often it had nowhere to work. One Monday morning in the old days, I arrived and found all my papers and files thrown into a corner and the office full of barrels of cement, paint and tools. Apparently some other department had decided to move in during the weekend! I went to see Mr Owen about it and will never forget seeing him also sitting surrounded by junk, calmly working away as if nothing had happened to disturb him! Of course, he had not had the decorative Miss Roche to help him in those days!

Eventually Colin Owen, who had done a great job as principal probation officer and had made friends of all races, reached his retirement age. Eric Hillier was posted from England to take over as our principal probation officer. Colin was almost broken-hearted and decided not to go back to the UK. Loving the country and the native people, he formed, from volunteer funds, the first Kenya Prisoners' Aid Society.

Meanwhile, I carried on supervising offenders on probation, trying to find them jobs and receiving progress reports from their employers. Interestingly, I got support from large employers such as the Heinz fresh foods canning factory at Kiambu, just outside Nairobi, and others.

*

One day, in the assistant probation officer's office, which was a little wooden shack in a murram compound far from the provincial HQ, the peace of the place was accentuated by the gentle scratching of the officer's pen and the dust gently blowing about around his door. The officer, a little man, stopped to polish his glasses …

Suddenly there was a martial tread outside and a gigantic retired major-general, who was farming in the district, sought admission. 'Good morning. My houseboy is far too busy to come to report today and so he asked me to come instead.'

'Have you got his book, sir?' enquired the officer.

The book was produced and the Major-General gazed down at the officer as he scratched something therein with his rusty pen.

Relaxing with a sigh, the diminutive officer returned the book and, looking up over his glasses, gravely requested, 'Please tell him to report here again on the 15th.'

'Thank you,' replied the Major-General, and the sound of his marching steps died away as the assistant probation officer resumed the scratching of a piece of paper with his relief nib.

Suddenly, the peace of the place was shattered again and the Major-General put his head round the door to enquire, 'When did you say I must report again?'

In his circular letter No. 54 of 15th November 1960, the principal probation officer ruled that probationers must report on time and in person. Reporting by proxy, by wives, cousins, brothers and sweethearts, was forbidden. Major-generals, however, were not specifically mentioned!

*

A little while later Eric Hillier fancied a holiday, was given six months' leave and went off to the Seychelles Islands, and I was, astonishingly, gazetted to act as principal probation officer with effect from 24th March 1961 (*Kenya Gazette* 4907)! Unfortunately Eric seemed to get the wind up and returned from leave five months later to carry on his substantive Colonial Office appointment.

The subject of 'Uhuru' and the era of independence of colonies had come to prominence in the early 1960s throughout the whole British Empire, and there was the usual Lancaster House conference where the future of Kenya was mapped out. In the first Kenyan self-government elections in 1963, the three main contestants were KANU (Kenya African National Union), headed by Jomo Kenyatta (recently released from prison), KADU (Kenya African Democratic Union), headed by Daniel arap Moi, and a party loosely headed by Jaramogi Oginga Odinga from the Jaluo, in the Kisumu area, and said to be financed by Soviet money.

A majority of the votes went to KANU, and Kenyatta was elected President. He immediately declared a one-party government, wisely naming his political contestant, Daniel arap Moi, Vice-President. Moi succeeded him on his passing with what can be described as a period of stable government. My sister-in-law Marion, who worked as secretary to Daniel arap Moi in the Education Department, said that he was one of the nicest men with whom she had worked.

After Jomo Kenyatta's release from trial and imprisonment in the remote Kapenguria area (he was described by the Governor as the leader of 'darkness and death'), he showed no signs of resentment, and when Freda and I met him on social occasions we found him remarkably affable.

During all this time, my father, who had so valiantly struggled with adversity to keep what was by then one of Kenya's oldest bookshops growing, had passed through the various ages of a man into his declining years. When he died at the age of eighty-six, on 22nd February 1962, he was still theoretically at the helm, although the course that he steered was not completely steady. My brother Harry, who had been working long and hard in the bookshop, wanted to emigrate to England with his wife Marion and son Peter. I, therefore, left the probation service in 1962 under the terms of the Limited Compensation Scheme in order to let him go to England.

After my brother Harry and my mother left Kenya, Freda and I ran the shop and found that most of our regular, mainly European, clients were leaving Kenya. This clientele purchased books and periodicals mainly imported from Britain. However, it became apparent that, if the shop was to survive, a new type of reading matter was required. Fortunately for us, the Colonial Office organisation which had supplied schools and colleges in Kenya with textbooks and writing materials did not seem to be interested in supplying the schools any more. This gap in the market was there to be exploited and we managed to get some big contracts to supply the schools with the textbooks and materials they required. Because of the contacts previously made in the transport and shipping concerns, we were able to provide quicker deliveries than they had experienced in the past.

In 1963 it was reported in the probation service newsletter that Mr Pius Oloo had been promoted to probation officer grade 1 in charge of the Rift Valley Province. Soon afterwards he wrote in his letter to me:

I am in no doubt aware of your commitments and that much confronts you to make a success of the shop and to keep it alive in memory of the late beloved father.

I have at last returned to Nakuru where you laid a foundation stone for this service and although there is quite much to handle I am happy to be back to it again.

For your information, Nakuru is not what it was during our time, there has been a remarkable progress made all over and the general look of the place is impressive. The case loads are not as high as they were in our time, with the exception of Eldoret which has the highest figure.

Pius and I continued to correspond with each other for many years. He told me of his move to Nyeri, which lies on the lower slopes of Mount Kenya. It was another cold place which did not suit him. Finally he was given a move to his beloved Kisumu in charge of Nyanza Province, from where I presume he retired.

It was shortly after this point that bookshop negotiations were commenced with Messrs E J Arnold & Son, who eventually became the major shareholder in the business. The archives of the business are very few, and it is presumed that not only did the management not regard them as being very valuable, but also much was destroyed in the two disastrous fires. However, in an old diary dated 1918, it is recorded that on the 12th November there was a 'peace' holiday, and on the 13th the takings were Rs (rupees) 149/35. Thereafter it is recorded that the 14th, 15th and 16th were also 'peace' holidays. It is a far cry from those old days, and the firm has grown with the protectorate and the crown colony and now finds itself a part of the nation, still with the name 'S J Moore'. When it was taken over by the present management, the new conservative African staff expressed fears that they would be discharged, but it was pointed out to them that a united company is a corporate body in itself, and their services would be retained with unbroken continuity. Moreover, in strengthening the financial resources of the company, their own security would be increased. Finally they could increase the potential of their own status by working hard to achieve promotion.

By this time both our sons, David and John, had completed their education and were at work in England, and Freda was anxious to see her mother again, so we packed up our belongings and bade farewell to Kenya, which had been our home for so many years, and set sail for England. We took the long way round Africa in order to see my sister Phoebe and Caspar in Durban, and then sailed in the *Edinburgh Castle* bound for Southampton. We were met at Waterloo station by David and his fiancée Carolyn, whom we met for the first time. Together we all travelled to Colchester, where we met the rest of the family.

Mount Longonot and sheep grazing.

Kenya coast.

Rural scene in Kenya – herding sheep and goats along a road.

Tim, surrounded by children, has captured their interest.

115

Postscript

꧁꧂

When Freda and Tim arrived back in England in 1967 they went to stay in Colchester with Freda's mother and aunt, and decided to look for a property of their own. They fairly quickly found a house under construction to their liking, which would have become their new home. However, fate decreed otherwise because Freda's mother and great-aunt died within a month of their arrival and, due to a variety of circumstances, they ended up living in the house in Colchester looking after Freda's aunt. Although the new house was completed, they never lived in it and eventually it was sold.

Tim got a job at the North East Essex Technical College in Colchester which he enjoyed and which he held until his retirement. He developed an interest in gardening and was quite successful in producing vegetables, although he had to take advice from the locals on when to sow seeds etc., not having had much experience of the British climate other than when on long leave. Tim's mother also joined the household from time to time on her wanderings around the various homes of her children.

After Freda's aunt and Tim's mother died, Freda and Tim were able to sell up the Colchester property and moved to Ringwood, Hampshire, to be halfway between where David and John were living on the south coast. Among the holidays they took at this time was a trip back to Kenya in 1982 which they both enjoyed. They eventually moved into sheltered accommodation. They were both actively involved in the church and social life in Ringwood.

After a short illness Freda died in October 1995 and Tim carried on alone in the flat, where he started writing this book. He died in September 2002.

Freda and Tim, July 1995.

Appendix I

◦◦◦

Report on Operations Against the Shifta on the Uebi Scebeli

Mogadishu

8 FEB. 44.

REPORT ON SHIFTA OPERATIONS ON THE UEBI SCEBELI IN JAN 1944.
Col P.R. MUNDY, DSO., OBE., MC., COMMANDING.
Map Ref. EAST AFRICA 1:500000 DOLO & EL FUD.

Before proceeding to recount in detail the movements of the various Shifta bands in this series of raids and the counter measures taken by Col. Mundy and the force under his command it is necessary to describe briefly the area in which the various actions took place, and the situation on the Uebi Scebeli immediately before the arrival of the main force of Somaliland Camel Corps (S.C.C.) and Somalia Gendarmerie (S.G.).

The area concerned is the Uebi Scebeli Valley stretching from Callafo to Imi. The country of the main raiding tribes – RER ABDILLE, RER AMADEN, RER ADEN KHEIR and others – lies to the North in the area between the River and EL FUD and westwards into Ethiopia across the DACATA. The tribe which suffers most from their depredations is the AULIHAN whose country lies to the South of the river, stretching down to EL CARRE and IET. In between these two main tribes, or groups of tribes, and along the river, there are the CARANLE, GHELIMES, SHEKAL and ABDULLA TALAMOGHE. The position of these tribes lying in the path of the raiding parties is, no doubt, somewhat unenviable, and it is certain particularly in the case of the GHELIMES and SHEKAL, that they act as spies for the raiding parties and report to them the movements of Gendarmeries Detachments.

The river itself, when full, offers an insuperable obstacle to the Shifta and raids can only be carried out with success in the dry season. Even when the river is low, there are only certain fords where camels can cross with any ease or safety. The line of the river, from Callafo to Imi is long and these fords are numerous, so that with only limited forces it is a difficult problem to choose which fords the Shifta will cross at with the looted stock, particularly when they possess an active band of spies all along the line of the river. It is no business of this report to

119

exaggerate the difficulties entailed in stopping the bands of Shifta on their outward or on their return journey, but taking into consideration the speed with which the Shifta move, even when accompanied with looted stock, and the possible choice of some twenty or more fords between CALLAFO and IMI, a very pretty problem faces anyone trying to stop all the bolt holes with limited forces. However careful he may be and however accurate and speedy may be the information brought by AULIHAN tribesmen, there remains a large element of chance in any operation.

The topography of the country North and South of the river confines to a certain extent the routes taken by the raiders. Raiders returning with looted stock generally appear to follow one of three main lines. First the valley of the DAUADID (JCK 0416) which route can be followed by crossing the Uebi Scebeli at MARUF (JCC 9297), CUGNO (JCD 0594), GABBA, HEIN DAB (JCD 2394) or DAGAHELA (JCD 2690). Secondly the valley of the MADDISO (JCK 4800) running North from ASHE GUDUD, or what is commonly called LUBB – the river crossings for this route being those of LUBB, FORARA, FARAH MAGOL or any of the numerous crossings near MELKA TAKA (JCD 5372). Thirdly a line approximating to that of the road running North to DANAN (JCL 1118) using the crossing at HARUNLE (BOHEL BAR) BAADLEI or GOLEI UAGA. On the South side of the river supplies of water are also confined to the areas of EL BAR (JCC 6873), DIGIBU (JCD 1069), DANAN DERE and DERCA DUR (JCD 3045) and the LABANSALE (JCD 8035), and Shifta bands will generally be found in those areas when preparing to re-cross the river with camels. It should be mentioned here, and this point will be emphasised later on, that any force has little chance of intercepting Shifta when on their outward journey. At this stage their main object is to reach the AULIHAN country as quickly as possible. They can, if necessary, move in very small parties and at great speed, and they are not confined to crossing the river at any ford. Naturally also they will avoid at all costs any action with Gendarmerie or other forces. On their return journey, however, conditions are different. Their speed is reduced; they must use certain fords, and they will offer action to any force in an effort to get their loot back to their own country.

To dignify the course of the Uebi Scebeli with the name of valley, is perhaps an unnecessary exaggeration. The country adjacent to this unwholesome stream is practically flat, and it is only at a distance of 10 miles or more that low hills appear. The river seems to support little vegetation – in some places meandering through typical African bush, whilst at others only the narrowest ribbon of trees is found. In many places large areas of completely bare sandy soil stretch away on either side of the river for a distance of 2–3 miles. The possible fertility of these alluvial deposits is no consolation when walking over them at midday.

It is unnecessary here to give in great detail the preliminary reports of this outbreak of raiding. The first news received was sent in two signals, one from

SEGAG and one from DAGHBUR, dated 11th Jan. and was to the effect that MALINGUR and AMADEN raiders were proceeding south in small parties intending to join up later and raid the AULIHAN country. 40 raiders had been seen in one party. On 18th Jan these reports were confirmed by a letter from Lieut. Carpenter at IMI in which he reported the presence of raiders in his area and gave his opinion that further large scale raids were about to commence. In view of this Lieut. Col. Collingwood, M.B.E. Senior Civil Affairs Officer, North West Province, who was then at Callafo, dispatched Lieut. Moore with one platoon to reinforce Lieut. Minnis at LUBB. The combined forces of Lieuts. Moore and Minnis then patrolled and watched in the LUBB-MELKA TAKA. On 18th Jan reliable information was obtained from Lieut. Minnis that approximately 300 raiders had crossed the river in several places between GABBA and MELKA TAKA, between 14th and 17th Jan. They were expected to re-cross in about 4 days. All available Gendarmerie reinforcements were immediately despatched in Motor Transport along the north bank to re-inforce MINNIS at MELKA TAKA and Capt. CORFE, Army Civil Affairs Officer, CALLAFO, proceeded along south bank with a force of Illaloes to contact that officer. Capt. Ryan O.C. Mounted Infantry Company, S.G. also arrived in CALLAFO on 18th Jan.

All the above information was received by the Commandant on the 18th Jan at MUSTAHIL which he had chosen as his H.Q. for Ex.Exchange. An immediate decision was made by him to utilise the forces at his disposal for Ex.Exchange ('A' and 'M' Squadrons. S.C.C.). The reliability of the reports concerning the projected raids and the fortunate presence of 2 Squadrons of well equipped S.C.C. with motor transport appeared to give good promise that this band of raiders might be intercepted and read a severe lesson. Accordingly at 1000 hrs on 19th Jan 'M' Squadron S.C.C. left Mustahil to re-inforce the Gendarmerie on the UEBI SCEBELI.

The intention of the Commandant was to block the return of the raiders by lining the river in their rear, and attacking them when they attempted to cross at the various fords. Any attempt at chasing them into the depths of the AULIHAN country would obviously have been futile.

On 20th Jan 'M' Squadron S.C.C. arrived at MELKA TAKA and contacted Capt. Ryan who had left Callafo on the 19th Jan with the new issue of .303 rifles, Bren guns and Sten guns for various detachments. All reports indicated that there were still approx 200 raiders on the SOUTH bank of the river, although a party of 20 had already succeeded in re-crossing to the North with their looted stock. It was also apparent that with the increased concentration of forces in the MELKA TAKA area, there was every probability that future attempts would be made in the vicinity of LUBB and the more westerly fords. Accordingly the Commandant decided that it would be necessary to re-inforce the detachments on the Uebi Scebeli with the remainder of the S.C.C. Detachment at Mustahil – A Squadron.

Therefore Force H.Q. and A Squadron left for Callafo at 1000 hrs on 21st Jan. By this time reports had come in of the actual raids. On 14th and 15th Jan substantial raids had taken place in the SCIELLELE and BUDDI areas (JBS 4895 and 7482) and on the 18th Jan raids had occurred on the AUDAMBOI plain (JCE 1544). These were by no means the last. It is interesting to note that during the period between 14th Jan and 21st Jan there were twelve authentic reports of raids carried out in the AULIHAN country South of the river. This does not take into account at least twice that number of reports which proved to be inaccurate or completely false.

By midday 21st Jan Force H.Q. and A Squadron had reached Callafo, here valuable information was given by Captain Todd, Army Civil Affairs Officer, GABREDARRE concerning the recent raids, and he reported that only the day before raids had occurred in the vicinity of GERREI (JCE 5033). Information was also received that Major Whaley (O.C. M Squadron) and Capt. Ryan were patrolling as far as IMI. On this day also Lieut Moore and Gendarmerie Detachment established themselves at BAADLEI. Force H.Q. and A Squadron proceeded as far as JCE 6528 and spent the night there. It was intended to establish Force H.Q. on the morrow at LUBB.

At this stage the situation on the river was as follows:-

1.	BAADLEI	Lieut. Moore and Detachment S.G.
2.	HARUNLE and vicinity	Lieut. Minnis and Detachment S.G.
3.	MELKA TAKA & vicinity	1 Troop M Squadron (mobile)
4.	LUBB	Detachment S.G.
5.	LUBB – IMI	1 Troop M Squadron (patrolling)

MELKA TAKA and LUBB areas were considered to be the most promising places for an attempted crossing.

The morning of 22nd Jan was uneventful for Force H.Q. and A Squadron which resumed their journey. A party of Illaloes from DANAN were contacted, but except for a plethora of irrelevant information and false directions emanating from their L/C, they had no news of value. Progress continued until 1200 hrs approx when the party stopped on the road opposite Baadlei. After a few minutes shots were heard coming from the river. Little time was lost in investigating their cause. After a brisk and warm march it was found that Lieut. Moore and his detachment had just finished a most successful action. A party of RER ABDILLE and ADEN KHIER numbering 75 approx with some 800 head of camels had attempted the ford. Result – all stock was recaptured and 5 Shifta were definitely killed with a strong probability of others killed and wounded, at the cost of one Gendarme slightly wounded. The attempt had been suspected by Lieut. Moore and a neat ambush had been affected. He was plentifully supplied with information concerning the movements of this band by AULIHAN Scouts, and his diary written in detail is full of interest. It would appear that it was a near thing as to whether a boil in the nose or this local operation would come to a head first.

As soon as the success of this action was apparent, the Commandant decided to reinforce Moore's detachment. Accordingly H.Q. A Squadron and 2 troops were placed at Baadlei and 1 troop was sent to GOLEI UAGA. It was at this stage felt that further attempted crossings would take place in this area. Force H.Q. then proceeded to HARUNLE and contact was made with Lieut. Minnis. He had nothing of importance to report, and camp was pitched near his position. During the early part of the night a patrol dispatched to watch DUSUBLE, contacted a few Shifta and some 20 camels. The former were dispersed and the latter subsequently collected. On 23rd Jan Force H.Q. proceeded on its way and contacted at 1000 hrs the troop of M Squadron watching the MELKA TAKA crossing. Here further good news was received. During the night a force of approx 40 Shifta had attempted to cross at KUBHANLEI with 300 head of stock. These ran into parties of Illaloes and Gendarmerie under Major Barry and Captain Corfe and were routed after a brisk action lasting about 30 minutes. The bulk of the stock was captured and 3 Shifta were wounded and 1 taken prisoner. It is likely that Shifta casualties would have been higher if the pin of a 36 Mills Grenade had not obstinately remained in situ after it had been thrown. In the early morning a further small party had attempted the crossing at DAGAHALE – result 1 Shifta wounded and all the camels – 24 – recaptured.

After the fords at MELKA TAKA and KUBHANLEI had been inspected Force H.Q. proceed to LUBB. On the morning of the 24th Jan information was obtained from local tribesmen that a party of Shifta numbering 20 with 100 head of stock had crossed at ARA GORA. An immediate patrol was dispatched to verify this and it proved unfortunately only too true. Owing to the lengthy start they had got it was felt to be useless to follow them. This news was signalled to GABREDARRE and SEGAG. Unfortunately this had to be done via Mogadishu. It should be stated here that all through these operations the lack of a direct signal link with the North was felt acutely. Major Whaley and Capt. Ryan returned to LUBB from their patrol to IMI, during the course of the morning, and the Commandant therefore decided to put into action the plan he had outlined. The reason for this was apparent. It was strongly felt that after the hot reception the Shifta had had on the more Easterly fords, future attempts would be made on the fords still further west than LUBB. To prevent this a striking force would operate on the South bank and endeavour to drive any Shifta whom it could not capture or kill towards the fords between BUR CALANE (FORARA) and GOLEI UAGA, which were strongly held. On this day Captain Garland and detachment from SEGAG and Lieut. Carpenter from IMI arrived at LUBB.

During the course of the day Captain Ryan and a detachment of Gendarmerie proceeded to the crossing at BUR CALANE and established a post there. In the early hours of the morning (25th) 1 Shifta and 9 camels crossed, and after pursuit the camels were recaptured and the Shifta wounded. This brings out the difficult problem confronting anyone attempting to ambush a Shifta at a ford. It is customary with them to send a small party of Scouts as a vanguard to test the ford, and the commander is faced with the decision whether to attack the first party coming through or to leave them in the hope that the main body will follow. In this case Captain Ryan allowed what he thought was a small scouting party through, and then the horrid realisation dawned on him that no more were to follow. Result, a pursuit at the double for some 6 miles. On the previous night also a small party had been intercepted at FARAH MAGOL just East of BUR CALANE and 30 camels recaptured, which tended to confirm the idea that generally the Shifta parties were moving westwards. In order to meet this Lieut. Carpenter and detachment were despatched in the evening to DAGAHALE 2, a ford some 10 miles west of LUBB.

On 25th Jan Ryan was reinforced and a standing patrol was established on BUR CALANE itself. This is a small eminence on the South bank of the river. It commands an extremely fine view of all the country to the South from opposite MELKA TAKA away to the West as far as GABBA. It was hoped that the dust raised by herds of looted stock could be observed and some forecast made of the ford for which they were making. No dust, however, was seen except that raised by numerous whirlwinds. The movements of the striking force were clearly visible from this hill and 4 lorries were spotted operating between MELKA TAKA and DENANE DERE. At 1500 hrs approx news was received at H.Q. from the striking force that they had contacted a large herd of camels – some 800 – accompanied by 50–60 raiders moving westwards from the MELKA TAKA area towards GABBA and MARUF. This force was judged at H.Q. to be the majority of the raiders then remaining on the South bank. Owing to night falling and very broken ground contact was lost by the striking force, and it appeared essential to adjust the existing arrangements, to meet the likelihood of this large force crossing in the vicinity of GABBA or MARUF. Accordingly Captain GARLAND and detachment were immediately sent to reinforce Lieut. Carpenter's detachment at DAGAHALE 2 and ARAGORA, and A Squadron were ordered to move westwards and hold as many of the fords in the area of HEIN DAB, GABBA, MARUF as possible. This was carried out with all speed and the bulk of A Squadron was in position by 1200 hrs 26th Jan. To fill the gap caused by the departure of A Squadron from the Eastern fords a signal was sent on 26th Jan to SEGAG (via Mogadishu) instructing O.C. Gendarmerie to send 2 motorised platoons via DANAN to GOLEI UAGA. The object of this force was to reinforce and expand Lieut. Moore's post at Baadlei and also to hold GOLEI UAGA. It was felt essential to call in this force in view of the information concerning further Shifta movements which was received subsequently on 26th Jan and which will be referred to later.

Evidence was not long in forthcoming that generally speaking the raiders were becoming demoralised and were splitting up into small parties. 'Sauve qui Peut' seemed to be becoming the order of the day. After the striking force lost contact with the large band referred to above, little further was heard of them and naturally there was much speculation as to the route they had taken. Later it became apparent that to a great extent this band must have dissolved into small parties, some with a few camels, attempting with partial success little known fords, others retiring to stretches of broken country inaccessible to Motor Transport in the hope that they might be able to cross after forces on the river had withdrawn – a somewhat forlorn hope considering the shortage of water in these areas.

During the night 25th–26th Jan AULIHAN entered the camp at LUBB with the welcome news that they had attacked a small party of Shifta somewhere South of ARAGORA. In proof of this 2 prisoners and 1 corpse were produced. The information obtained from the prisoners definitely confirmed the conclusions referred to above. In addition they stated that one BUTHUL GALAYA (Rer Timas), a Shifta leader and one known to have organised previous raids had been killed in one of the actions at KUBHANLEI or BAADLEI.

During 26th Jan. news was received from Baadlei that further attempts by small parties to cross had been made; these had been repulsed and 1 Shifta had been wounded. The striking force patrolled the DENANE DERE and MARUF areas, but no contact was made. News, however, was received that a further large band of Shifta numbering about 30 with some 400–500 head of stock were approaching LABANSALE from BUDDI. Arrangements were being made for their reception by the striking force.

It can be seen at this juncture that the situation was not without its complications. It might have seemed at first a fairly simple operation to line the river crossings and dispatch the striking force to the Southern bank, rather in the manner of inserting a ferret into a rabbit warren. The results, however, were not so simple, and it was no easy task to follow accurately the movements of the many Shifta bands, or to form quickly a correct picture of what exactly was happening in the extensive area in which they were manoeuvring. There was also the added anxiety caused by seemingly endless supply of new and hitherto unknown fords, for which detachments had to be found.

During the night 26th to 27th Jan 15 raiders with 80 camels slipped across at FARAH MAGOL. This party was hotly pursued by Capt. RYAN and Lieut. Hobhouse and after 20 miles had been covered at high speed, the camels were recaptured and one Shifta wounded. At 11.30hrs 27th Jan, news was received from

A Squadron that troops had been posted at HEIN, DAB, GABBA, and SUNKATFIN and a patrol was proceeding to MARUF. Otherwise they had little to report. At 1800 hrs the striking force reported that they had contacted a large number of camels – 250 with 20–30 Shifta – some 14 miles from MELKA TAKA. 230 camels were recaptured and the Shifta dispersed. This was obviously the band reported to be moving to LABANSALE from BUDDI on the 26th.

28th Jan brought the news that a party of 4 Shifta had been encountered near GABBA and one had been killed and one wounded. A party also of unknown strength had attempted the crossing at KUBHAMLEI and at HURANLE, but had been driven off. During the day information was brought to Force H.Q. at LUBB by AULIHAN tribesmen that a party of Shifta with some 80 camels were 'lying up' at 8 miles south of LUBB. A force was sent from LUBB to deal with these, and 70 camels were recaptured. On this day further news was received from the striking force concerning the whereabouts of the Shifta band with whom contact had been lost on 25th Jan. They were reported as being in the area of WAYAH (JCC 9570) and EL BAR. Therefore a widespread sweep of this area and that of DENANE DERE was organised whilst at the same time foot patrols from A Squadron were to proceed South of the river.

On the early morning of the 29th Jan a detachment of A Squadron seized 70 camels at a ford near GABBA and later 100 camels were recaptured by the striking force in the course of their sweep. Contact was also established on this day between A Squadron and Capt. McDowell of the Mounted Infantry at IMI. All the information received on the 30th Jan suggested that the Shifta had become completely disorganised. 20 Shifta and 30 camels, a significant proportion effected a crossing near GABBA, but lost 7 camels in the river by doing so. A further party of 5 Shifta were encountered at FORARA of which one was killed and one wounded. It is unnecessary to continue to chronicle these small actions. Clearly the bulk of the looted stock had been recaptured, the raiders dispersed and the task accomplished. The Commandant therefore decided to withdraw the S.C.C. detachment at Mustahil, while the Mounted Infantry and El Carre detachments of the Gendarmerie returned to their respective stations. This movement started on 31st Jan. On that day Force H.Q. and A Squadron withdrew to MELKA TAKA, the striking force withdrawing independently along the South bank. A small details camp was established there where the various Gendarmerie Sub-Units could be re-organised. On 1st Feb the Force continued to withdraw to Callafo. On the way CATFORCE from SEGAG was contacted. It will be remembered that this force had already been instructed to assist in holding the Eastern fords. This force was established at MELKA TAKA. On return to Mustahil (2nd Feb) news was received from SEGAG that it was possible that a further outbreak of raiding might begin. 380 Shifta were reported to be moving South from the vicinity of EL FUD. It was felt at the time that this report might be exaggerated, but in order to guard against any possible recurrence M Squadron was ordered to remain at Callofo temporarily to assist Catforce if necessary. Up to the present date no more raids have been reported.

It will be seen from the foregoing account of these operations that the results were most successful. It is safe to say that some 2000 camels were recaptured, if the number collected independently by the AULIHAN is included, and some 30 Shifta were either killed, wounded or captured. This force of raiders has been taught a severe lesson, and the reports which they will undoubtedly carry back to their homes of the numbers – no doubt greatly exaggerated – and strength of the S.C.C. and Gendarmerie forces should have most beneficial results. It is proper here to stress most strongly that the successful conclusion to this operation and all the good effects it may have were entirely due to the Commandant's decision at the outset to utilise the whole 'Wario' force, destined for Ex. Exchange, as a punitive force against the Shifta. It does not require very much imagination – none at all for those who were present – to see that the forces normally engaged in this area, i.e. the Mounted Infantry Company, Somalia Gendarmerie and the detachment from EL CARRE under Lieut. MINNIS would have been even with their local knowledge and customary energy, hopelessly overburdened in this task through sheer lack of numbers. In addition at this season of the year there is little or no grazing on the Uebi Scebeli, and thus it was impossible for the Mounted Infantry Company to use their animals, and their movements and chances of success were gravely hampered. The addition of the 2 Squadrons of the S.C.C. and their excellent transport and the 15 G.T. Trucks allocated for the Exercise changed a most unsatisfactory situation into a most promising one.

The conclusions which can be drawn from these operations are simple, and they will, no doubt, be echoed by all Gendarmerie Officers who have been engaged in the past in this area and who are in a position to judge. First, the Gendarmerie forces available to patrol and police this area and to subdue Shifta activity are ludicrously inadequate. This may be unpleasant hearing but it remains a fact, which cannot be altered by any talk of expediency or juggling with the existing Gendarmerie forces. The valley of the Uebi Scebeli from Callafo to Imi and the surrounding districts in which the Shifta operate form an area of 7,000 square miles. This, of course, does not include the SEGAG-DACATA, EL CARRE and ODDO districts. This vast area is very largely peopled by turbulent tribes who resort to raiding as a matter of course, when their economic situation becomes acute. Into it, also from Ethiopia are spewed continually both weapons and further tribesmen of an even more restless and intractable nature. Further there is little doubt that this 'export trade' is vigorously encouraged by the individuals who are styled as Ethiopian officials. The Abyssinian campaign has furnished anyone who was fortunate enough to take part in it, with ample evidence of the rapacity, malice and aggressiveness of the ruling caste in this so called 'Empire'.

Taking into consideration all this, an expansion of the Gendarmerie by 3 companies for use in the Shifta infected area becomes a necessity. It is also urged that every effort should be made to equip the Gendarmerie with 'JEEPS' and Mortars, both 2" and 3". The value of the latter in bush warfare is well known, and the former would be of untold value for their cross country qualities, speed and toughness. (The appalling state of the road along the Uebi Scebeli caused numerous breakdowns in the motor transport used in this operation, and normal motor transport in such conditions works under a very great handicap.)

The second conclusion is that a thorough disarming campaign should be started at once in the RER AMADEN country and that of the adjacent clans. As will have been seen from this report, the majority of the raiders have succeeded in retaining their arms and returning, if empty handed, to their country. They have had a lesson, but it is useless to imagine it will be a lasting one while they have weapons – which no doubt will be speedily augmented – and while the economic causes of their raiding continue. Prompt and efficient disarmament [would] certainly have far more happy and lasting results than a dozen successful operations such as the one described.

This report would not be complete without mention of the raising of the morale of the Gendarmerie personnel by the recent issue of the new .303 rifles, Bren Guns, Sten Guns and Grenades. Anyone who has tried to bring about a high standard of efficiency with cast-off Italian equipment will readily understand this.

Finally it must be said how greatly the hard work of Major Withycombe, S.C.C. and his Adjutant Lieut. CORDWENT and Major Whaley of M Squadron are appreciated; the administrative problems arising in this operation were considerable, and the solving of them was largely due to the pains taken by these Officers and indeed by all Officers of the S.C.C. and Gendarmerie. Special mention must also be made of the fine work done by Captain RYAN and Lieut. MOORE, the latter in one action seizing nearly half the total of recaptured stock. And lastly, the drivers of the G.T. vehicles allocated for the exercise, who, no doubt, expected tarmac roads and routine journeys, but who found themselves in very different surroundings, and who with few exceptions, despite their inexperience, acquitted themselves well.

(SIGNED............R.A.RUSSELL SMITH)
CAPTAIN,
ASST STAFF OFFICER,
for COLONEL, COMMANDANT,
SOMALIA GENDARMERIE.

❧ *Appendix I* ☙

<u>Abbreviations used in the report</u>

S.C.C.	Somaliland Camel Corps
S.G.	Somalia Gendarmerie
O.C.	Officer Commanding
.303 rifles	P40 (Lee Enfield Mark 4), 0.303" calibre rifles
G.T. vehicles	General Transport, i.e. not armoured

Appendix II

୧୷୶ଡ଼

Letters from Somalia

January 28th 1944
Gabredarre

Dear Moore,

I have heard through Major Barry and Corfe that you and your men have had a scrap with the Shifta and hit them with a good crack and recaptured several hundred camels; a jolly good show!! This is just a short note to offer you my congratulations, and your men too. I have not yet had full particulars of the engagement; if you write a report on it, I would be most interested to have a copy, if you have got one spare, or you can get Luigi at Callafo to type one out for you. Now that the Colonel is on the scene, and has brought the Camel Corps with him, we are anxiously awaiting further news to hear that the Shifta have been engaged again and knocked for six. Please thank your men from me and tell them how pleased I was to hear that your force had done so well, and that I hope that they will have further opportunities of hitting the shifta even harder.

Cheers and all the best,
Yours sincerely
F W V Collingwood.[1]

*

---

[1] Lieutenant Colonel Collingwood obviously overlooked that his orders, in No Secret/7/220 of 13th January 1944, were not followed!

R.W. Ryan Capt.
O.C. 'D' Coy (Mounted Infantry)
Somalia Gendarmerie
Mogadishu
15/2/44

Dear Mrs Moore,

Perhaps you will remember me, and perhaps not! Any way I thought I'd like to write and tell you that Timmy your son was attached to my Coy. for a short while during January, and that while with us he fought an action against a superior number of enemy, and defeated them, killing 5 and wounding about 10–15 more, and recapturing about 800 camels that they had raided. In fact he did a really excellent job of work and the C.O. was very pleased with him, not to mention myself, who am naturally very pleased, as the men Timmy had are of my Coy. and he handled them and the whole scrap in a really fine way.

Timmy and his platoon were one of a number of parties put at ford on the river, to lay and intercept a large bunch of Shifta which we knew were trying to cross with stolen stock.

The biggest lot of Shifta, about 100 men, nearly all armed, chose Timmy's ford to cross at. He laid an excellent ambush and defeated the enemy by his surprise attack, and captured almost all the camels. I just thought that you would like to know this, as, having known Timmy for some years, I am sure he will not make much of this incident when he tells you about it!

I have tried hard to get him posted to my company but I am afraid I have not succeeded, but time will tell.

His coolness and pluck were the main factors towards the success of the fight I have mentioned.

I believe he would like to come to this Coy. so perhaps we can work it between us.

All the best for 1944.

Yours very sincerely
Bill Ryan.

PS. Timmy only lost 1 man who was wounded and is recovering I think.

*

Lieut. D.G. Drysdale,
Somalia Gendarmerie HQ,
Mogadishu, Somalia,
2 Nov. 44

Dear Tim,

Many thanks for your two letters – I am most distressed to hear you are ill – get better and then be sensible and come back to the Gendarmerie again. McKillium is doing your job at the moment and spends his time sending notes beginning 'Lieut Drysdale will……….' depressing, and apart from this there is now no one to take me out for walks and I am growing fat and disagreeable – I shall have to take some 'Bob Martin's'.

The news since you left is not really worthy of note – I was under a cloud for a time after having shot some Ethiopian soldiers by mistake, but that has blown over.

John has come back as a Major, but looks much the same after four drinks as he did as a Captain.

Sloane has gone down to Kenya, where he will probably be certified – he went quite mad on me towards the end.

Segag you would not recognise and looks like a beach-head in France on 'D' day – everything is very war-like and one can't even walk up the hill without being challenged by three different sentries. Thank goodness I am away out at Geldoh where we are not troubled by it all. Dagabur is terrifying – Aeroplanes, D.I.Ds., Signals – they actually hold cinema shows twice a week! Troops all over the place. The shifta? – everyone is too busy to worry about them at all!

My Company Commander is now Arnold Berry – he is not so well disciplined as Sloane but I think I shall be able to lick him into shape in time.

Basil is well and you will probably see him shortly as he going down on leave.

I think that is more or less all that has been going on and 'should put you in the picture, actually'.

I am really very comfortable at the moment – as I say we are at Geldoh, but we have tents and a wireless set (the kind you have in the mess, not the kind that sends ciphers, although we have one of those too). The rains are just coming to an end, although they don't make much difference – we just dismiss smartly to our tents with a bottle of gin and stay there until it stops.

Dust devils are rather a problem – they come into camp with a look of anticipation on their faces – have a look around, spot a likely tent, usually the office – gather speed – and then go through it.

I have already lost two handkerchiefs, a pair of shorts and a secret cipher document.

The only indigenous inhabitants of Geldoh at the moment are a family of ground squirrels – there are baby ones and they are all becoming quite tame – I feed them twice a day with nuts. I don't know what they will do when we go, because I can't think what they could find to eat here if we didn't feed them.

I have been able to do quite a bit of sketching here – nothing startling, but I am quite satisfied. I trust you are continuing with your water colours because I expect to see some good stuff if and when I see you again. I wish you were here so that we could compare notes – it does make such a difference.

Having, I am quite convinced, said nothing whatsoever of interest, I will end because it is time to listen to the wireless. After we have had the Somali programme for the troops, the Swahili programme for the signallers, and the Italian programme for the dresser (we have an Italian dresser, quite a nice one who shaves) it leaves about half an hour for us, to which we look forward all day.

All the best Timmy, get better, write again, and do come back.

Yours,
Gordon.
P.S. Arnold sends his regards and wishes you well again.

*

A C A O[2] Duhun,
Ogaden Province,
Somalia,
16/2/46

Dear Timmy,

I have been here nearly a month now and am quite settled in. I wonder if you remember Duhun, it is 50 miles from Segag on the eastern side of the Kara Jaka hills. My own house, of the mud and wattle variety, stands on a small hill overlooking the business part of the station. The village, such as it is, a few dukas and huts is about ½ mile away. As luck would have it, I had a dose of fever whilst visiting Segag last week. I was laid up for seven days; rather a bore. I thought I had got rid of my Malaria, not having had an attack for nearly 2 years.

About the tribal map. A new one has been brought out and I will try and get hold of a spare copy to send you, most of the old Eytie ones seem to have vanished from this corner of the Ogaden.

There is no raiding or trouble of any sort at the moment.

Jerry Stanley, now a Major, is running the Somalia Courier in Mogadishu. Jock Gordon asked to be remembered to you and sends his kind regards.

Give my best wishes to your wife, mother and father.

Cheerio for now
Bruce (Minnis)

---

[2] Army Civil Affairs Officer

HEADQUARTERS,

1ST EAST AFRICAN INFANTRY BRIGADE,

NAIROBI.

LIST OF KIT TO BE CARRIED BY BRITISH RANKS.

Bde. H.Q. is liable to move at 12 hours notice and set out hereunder is a list of personal kit which every British rank is expected to provide for himself.

The scale of baggage (300 lbs.) for each British rank includes an allowance of 50 lbs. for mess stores.

The European War Establishment of Bde. H.Q. is as follows:-

W.E.	Actual Strength on 25/9/39.
Commander (Brigadier)	Brig. J.A. Campbell, D.S.O.
Brigade Major,	Capt. R.B. Pembroke.
Staff Captain,	Capt. C.H. O'Reilly.
Intelligence Officer,	2/Lieut. C.W.E. Buchanan.
Transport Officer,	Pte. J.D. Knight.
3 Cypher Officers,	2/Lieut. R.L. Oak-Rhind,
	Pte. D.H. Creed Newton,
	W.O.II. S.G. Clutton.
Orderly Officer,	Lieut. A.B. Tannahill.
5 British Clerks,	W.O.I. D. Dewar,
	W.O.II. S.J. Moore
	(three short).
1 British C.Q.M.S.	A/C.Q.M.S. C.R. Spiers.

CLOTHING.

2 Bush shirts	Khaki shirts & singlets within reason
3 prs. shorts	1 pr. khaki slacks.
1 pr. puttees	2 prs. khaki stockings
3 prs. socks	1 great coat or macintosh
2 prs. boots	1 pr. shoes
1 helmet	2 prs. pyjamas
handkerchiefs	towels.

EQUIPMENT.

1 camp bed	1 camp chair
1 mosquito net	1 camp basin
blankets & bed-clothes	1 camp bath
	1 hurricane lamp
1 camp table	1 electric torch
1 canvas bucket	Military equipment including water
1 charcoal iron	bottle.

TOILET GEAR.

Razor	Tooth brush
Shaving brush	tooth paste
Shaving soap	Toilet soap
Hair brushes	Washing soap
Toilet paper	quinine, aspirin, etc.
Cleaning material	(including boot polish & brushes,
Shaving Mirror.	clothes brush)

1 CHOP BOX CONTAINING:-

If you do not have any do NOT buy any as it is hoped to arrange for a Mess Chop box

1 Frying pan	1 Enamel soup plate
2 sufferias	2 Enamel meat plates
1 small kettle	3 knives, 3 forks, 3 spoons
1 Enamel mug	

- 2 -

Each British rank should arrange for a personal boy
(with knowledge of cooking if possible).   Attestation papers
in duplicate are attached hereto for particulars to be entered
by you. In the event of moving into the field they will
be enlisted as African followers.

Captain,

for STAFF CAPTAIN,
1ST EAST AFRICAN INFANTRY BRIGADE.

NAIROBI,   27th. September, 1959.

SOMALIA GENDARMERIE.

HANDING AND TAKING OVER CERTIFICATES.

I certify that I have taken over from/handed over to:—

(name) _2/Lt S. J. Moore._

the command/~~charge of~~ (Station, Company or Platoon):—

Callafo, S. Gendarmerie Detachment

and that all arms, ammunition, equipment, stores and rations are correct.

I have also taken over/~~handed over the keys of safe~~, cash Shs. (in words) _Nil_

pay documents, all registers, books, correspondence files, returns and the last Inspection Report.

The found articles, including seized arms and ammunition, and the Lost and Found Property Book have been checked and are correct.

Any exceptions to be entered hereunder:

Allen Capt.
_R.P.O._

....
Receiving Officer.

....
Handing Over Officer.

Dated _23/9/42._

Copy to the Commandant, Gendarmerie.
One copy to be filed at the Station.
One copy to be kept by Relieving Officer.
One copy to be kept by Officer relieved.

Interference from a civil affairs officer

137

OCCUPIED TERRITORY ADMINISTRATION
SOMALIA

SUBJECT T.T. POLICE. C/O S. GENDARMERIE

Ref. No.

To:- Mr. s.J. Moore Liutenant

Date 4th october 1943

Salam sana baada ya

salam. Nakwalifu barua ili kutaka hali yako kama hujambo, na mimi huku sijambo. Safari yangu nimefika salama pamoja na wetu wangu nilio kuwanao ndani ya safari. Bwana captain aliye kuwa in charge wa canvoy alitufanyia heshima kubwa kwakila kitu tulichohitaji tuliweza kupata bila shaka yoyote. tunamshukul u sana kwa wema wake na mungu amsaidie katika kazi yake.

Bwana tafadhali sana kwa wema wako na utukufu wako , unisamehe san nimechelewa kuku letea barua kwa sababu nilipofika Mogadishu, sikuweza kupata nafasi hata kidogo kwa kazi ilikuwa nyingi sana.

Na sasa nina fanya kazi ya (H.M. PRISONS) pamoja na Bwana Major E.R. GARNER. superintendent of prisons Mogadishu.

Naenderea vizuri na kazi yangu. Nilionana na Bwana virgin wa NO 1 N.W.P. Gabredarre yeye sasa ndiyo liutenant: aliniuliza habari ya leave yangu na mimi nika mwambiya ni nzuri.

Naema aliniambiya kwamba Bwana S.J. Moore atarudi katika nchi hii somalia malingine mimi napenda sana kama wewe utarudi kwa sababu mimi nataka kama utakuja nataka tukae pamoja kama zamani. namna ya callafo N.W.P. Basi Bwana sina maneno mengi ila hayo

kwaheli sasa nikipata nafasi nitakuletea barua ingine.

R.89 C.S.M. *Kitura*
T.T. POLICE.
SOMALIA GENDARMERIE C.P.S.
MOGADISHU.

This letter from CSM Kitura begins with extensive greetings following his arrival in Mogadishu. He is now working for HM Prisons with Major E R Garner, and everything is going well. Bwana Virgin is now a lieutenant, who asked him for news of his leave, which was good.
He asks if Bwana S J Moore will return to Somalia because he would like to work together as before. Finally he asks how Callafo and NWP (North Western Province) are, then writes, 'Goodbye and I will write again.'
It should be noted that CSM Kitura was from Tanganyika, which was previously German East Africa. His parents' generation would have been the first to see white Europeans, and here he has used a typewriter and written a letter in a foreign language: KiSwahili.

BRITISH MILITARY ADMINISTRATION
SOMALIA

Refce. No. Secret/7/220

Office of the
Senior Civil Affairs Officer
North Western Province
on tour at Callafo.
January 13th. 1944 SOMALIA
Date

TO Lt. Moore
Somalia Gendarmerie
Callafo.

With reference to the attached copy of letter which arrived for
Captain Ryan this morning from Lt. Carpenter at Marca the following
telegram reached me last night from Sagag.
      TO Dagahbur rptd Gabredarre
      FROM Sagag   IMPORTANT   dated 11th. T.O.O. 11-10 hrs
Gendarmerie and Civaffairs (.) Malingur and Amaden raiders left for
Aulihan 9th. (.) 40 seen in party, more believed joining (.) Travelling via GELDOH (.) Illaloes leaving with Stephenson to inform McDowell.
             ----

2.   Major Barry and Captain Corfe left this morning to inform El Car
-re taking two trucks and a party of Illaloes, with instructions to
reinforce Lt. Carpenter as quickly as possible from El Carre.
3.   It is known that Lt Minnis was at Lab on January 10th but
the strength of his patrol is not known, and it is possible that he
sent some of his men to reinforce Carpenter.
4.   You will proceed immediately with trucks B.M.A.S. 128 and 133
to reinforce Lt. Minnis at Lab taking with you
Gendarmer:2 L.M.Gs and 26 men. also two drivers and Sgt mechanic
Ibrahim.
        The whole party including the drivers is rationed up to and
including January 28th.
5.   You will find Lt. Minniss and place yourself under his orders
and work as one combined strong patrol on the Webi Schebelli and
its fords. It may well be that Major Mason kxxx and some of the
A.F.Vs have already engaged these shifta xnd or are hard on their
tails. On no account are you to engage any party of shifta which
is estimated to be xxxxxxxxxxxxxxxxxxxx in much greater strength
than your own force. If possible, get into communication with Imi and
El Carre by using civilian messengers and paying them, and exchange
information. I do not wish to cramp your style, but if you and Minnis
with your combined force meet a party of shifta which you are
confident that you can engage with every chance of success, then hit

BRITISH MILITARY ADMINISTRATION
SOMALIA

Office of the

them hard.

On the other hand if you get news of a force in considerably greater strength than your own, who are returning from a raid with large herds of stolen stock, then you should endeavour to get SOMALIA information to the other Gendarmerie units in the Imi area, and at the same time follow and if possible, harrass Date the raiders, without getting yourselves seriously involved in a major engagement. Always bear in mind the tactics of the shifta in the recent engagements whereby they have come in on the flanks and rear; if you get involved in an engagement you must carefully watch xttxfxxxxx your front, both flanks and rear.

6. You must use your own judgment regarding the trucks. I would like them back when Lt Minnis thinks that they can reasonably be spared. If xxx on arrival you hear that Major Mason has already engaged the shifta and they have been dispersed and the countryside is reasonably quiet, then the trucks should be returned to Callafo.

Lt. Colonel
Senior Civil Affairs Officer
North Western Province.

Copy to Lt; Minnis Somalia Gendarmerie.

The order from Lt Col. Collingwood referred to at the beginning of Chapter 5, which came too late for events on the ground!

SOMALIA

Date   13 FEB. '48.

    Capt. S.J. MOORE served with the Somalia Gendarmerie
from 15th June 1941 until the 30th July 1944.

    This Officer shows keenness and great attention to duty. He
is accurate in his work and shows good judgment.

    He acted as Administrative Officer to a Group Commander for
four months, which duties he carried out to the satisfaction of
his Superior. During operations in the Uebi Shebelli area in 1943
he carried out his work in a highly satisfactory manner.

                                                 COLONEL,
                                              COMMANDANT.

PRM/MG/Dict.   SOMALIA GENDARMERIE.

141

From P.O.Box 350, Nakuru.
8th July, 1953.

To all Members of "A" Force,
Special Police,
NAKURU.

Dear Moore

    With effect from the 7th July, 1953, the Superintendent of
Police, Rift Valley Province, has agreed to a temporary "stand down"
of the Special Police, Nakuru, and the Asian Home Guard.

    This means that, until further notice, your duties in "A" Force
will cease, unless there is need for a special call out. There will
be no further need for any night duty at the Town Hall.

    However, one duty does remain and that is to guard the
Hospital. This is most important as the Hospital staff are almost
exclusively female and the patients unable to protect themselves.

    We, together with "B" Force and "C" Force have been asked
to do this duty, which consists of three men a night from 9.30 p.m.
to 6 a.m. the next morning, taking turns. If enough men can be
found to take part in this duty, it should only come round about
once every 3 weeks or so. Will you please, therefore, complete
and return to me the attached slip as quickly as possible.

    Thank you for your help and co-operation in the past, which
I am sure you will willingly give in the future also.

Yours faithfully,

(L.E. LONG)
Commander "A" Force
Special Police
Nakuru.

*When the emergency was declared in October 1952 a number of civilians were recruited into a
'Home Guard'. However, it was soon realised that the Mau Mau were not interested in attacking
anyone in the town, being far outside the Kikuyu tribal area, and this special force was allowed to
quietly disappear.*